The
Theory & Practice
of
Travel

The
Theory & Practice
of
Travel

KEITH WATERHOUSE

Hodder & Stoughton
LONDON SYDNEY AUCKLAND TORONTO

Illustrated with cartoons by Alex Graham

British Library Cataloguing in Publication Data

Waterhouse, Keith, *1929–*
   The theory and practice of travel.
   1. Travel
   I. Title
   910.4

   ISBN 0-340-42500-8

First published in Great Britain 1989

Published by Hodder and Stoughton,
a division of Hodder and Stoughton Ltd,
Mill Road, Dunton Green, Sevenoaks, Kent TN13 2YE
Editorial Office: 47 Bedford Square, London WC1B 3DP

Photoset by Rowland Phototypesetting Ltd,
Bury St Edmunds, Suffolk

Printed in Great Britain by
T. J. Press (Padstow) Ltd, Padstow, Cornwall

For my part, I travel not to go anywhere, but to go. I travel for travel's sake. The great affair is to move.

ROBERT LOUIS STEVENSON

ITINERARY

THE
ARMCHAIR
TRAVELLER

The
Theory & Practice
of
Travel

KEITH WATERHOUSE

Hodder & Stoughton

25 Excuses for Staying Put

Y ou could be bumped off the flight –
        That's if the airline computer has ever heard
of you.

The air traffic controllers at Barcelona could be on strike.

The luggage tags for Geneva (GVA) and Guatemala (GUA) are dangerously similar – who knows where your bags might end up?

Isn't the House of Commons holding some kind of enquiry into air safety?

And according to what you've read in the papers, we're about due for another hijack.

Someone might plant drugs on you.

Wasn't there something on the news about freak hurricanes on the way?

The neighbours went there last year and didn't think much of it.

The world out there is crawling with clever handbag thieves.

It may seem quiet at the moment, but don't you remember when there were students hurling cobbles and the riot police using tear gas?

The courier might not be there to meet you at the other end –

And even if she is, you'll spend the next two weeks worrying in case she doesn't turn up with the airport minibus when it's time to come home.

You could arrive to find a message that the cat's gone missing.

Maybe your room will still have the builders in.

When the hotel takes your passport, you may never get it back again.

Inflamed by the foreign temperature, your partner could fall foolishly and passionately in love with a gigolo/adventuress.

You could be in for a bad case of Gyppy Tummy.

You could get lost and not be able to remember the name of your hotel.

The way their coaches drive, it's surprising even more of them don't plunge over a ravine while negotiating a hairpin bend at speed.

Maybe your room will still have the builders in

A bite from one of the insects they have over there could turn into something really nasty.

And don't you remember that film *So Long at the Fair*, where Jean Simmons's brother gets cholera so the concierge and her husband brick up his room and swear blind they've never set eyes on him?

Don't they throw you into the stinking jail first and ask questions afterwards if you get involved in even the slightest car accident in some of these countries?

What if the brigands who ambush you and threaten to cut off your ear won't accept American Express?

Then there's always rabies.

On the other hand . . .

11

Passport & Credentials

I have been a traveller since the age of three, when I toddled off down the street to find out what lay around the corner. That adventure, while short and ultimately unpleasant (my curiosity was rewarded with a scolding), encapsulates the purpose of travel so far as I am concerned. It is to reach the rainbow's end. Whether it leads me to a crock of gold or a cowpat is not wholly material. The object is to be somewhere else, to see what it's like.

From that early exercise in wanderlust, I have remained a happy victim of the travel bug. As a schoolboy my favourite expedition was through a storm drain at the edge of the park, leading out into a housing development of no interest even to those who lived in it. No matter: I was somewhere else, and that made it an Alice in Wonderland expedition.

As a young estate agent's clerk whose rent-collecting duties each Monday took up rather less of the working day than my employers imagined, I would take myself off on bus rides to the nearby mill towns – Huddersfield, Halifax, Dewsbury, to eat sticky buns in milk bars identical to the one back home in Leeds. But I wasn't back home, that was the point: I was elsewhere, where the air was headier, the soot sootier, and the buns stickier.

And sometimes I would take the tram to the Leeds and Bradford boundary, marked by a hundred yards of cinder track where the Leeds tram system left off and the Bradford system began. Walking across that crunching no-man's-land was for me like crossing through Checkpoint Charlie – and indeed when I did come to cross through Checkpoint Charlie for the first time it reminded me of nothing so much as the Leeds–Bradford tram interchange, where the feeling of entering foreign territory was so overwhelming that I would feel let down not to find frontier posts and passport control.

So it was as an already seasoned traveller that, in those days of conscription, I signed up in the RAF with every hope of getting my knees brown in

Malaysia or at the very least my feet cold in West Germany. In the event, the farthest I got was Bridgnorth, Shropshire, and I never saw an aeroplane on the ground in my whole two years before the windsock. Still, I did travel to faraway places: to Lancashire, North Yorkshire, Gloucestershire, Oxfordshire; and each hamlet or market town encountered was ringed on my mental map as another spot been to. I had a yearning to be posted to Middle Wallop just to say I'd been there, but it was not to be.

I did, however, realise another ambition, and that was to see London. I saw London three or four times, as a matter of fact, staying at the Union Jack Club in Waterloo for a few coppers a night. I came to regard myself as something of a cosmopolitan. While I didn't claim to know the capital like the back of my hand, I knew how to get about – you caught the tube. If it wasn't on the tube, you didn't go. But the three parts of London I most wanted to see, because I had read about them in novels, eluded me – Mayfair, Chelsea and Soho. None of them was on the tube map, and Chelsea and Soho didn't even figure on the Monopoly board. Not caring to accost strangers with the question, 'Excuse me, could you direct me to Soho?', I was reduced to aimless wanderings in search of these exotic locations. In a fog thicker than any London pea-souper, I was nevertheless in my element, drinking in the sights and sounds and smells of the capital; but it was not until I settled in it that I learned that Soho was not, as I had imagined, somewhere in the East End. (I think I had it mixed up with Limehouse.)

I had pined for London: now, living there, I pined to be abroad. Luckily my chosen trade of journalism was one with reasonable expectations in this direction. The first place beyond these shores I was despatched to was Dublin. Not *quite* abroad – but I was so eager for Eire to be in foreign parts that when addressing my postcards home I painstakingly copied out the Gaelic form for England, as one puts *Angleterre* when writing from France. But soon I was to get my first real foreign assignment: to the island of Bornholm in the Baltic, reached by ferry from

Copenhagen. I can still conjure up the sweet smell of woodsmoke from the herring-curing plant; I drank it in like a Bisto kid. Yes, this was foreign ground all right. I was so enchanted by the foreignness of it all – the strange coins, the traffic driving on the right, the comic opera policemen, Copenhagen's yellow single-decker trams, and the taste of cold lager and aquavit, that the story I had come for (dissidents escaping from Poland by pedalo) seemed rather dull in comparison, and it was with some reluctance that I abandoned my café table overlooking the square to chase it up.

My first visa was for Spain. I was enormously proud of it and kept ogling it all the way to Madrid. After that, as my passport began to fill up with rubber-stamped oblongs and squares and triangles (what a shame most European countries don't stamp your passport any more), I began to fancy myself a globetrotter. The gaudy stickers on my typewriter case – Cyprus, Jordan, Israel, West Africa, as well as just about every European country – proclaimed to the world that I was a much-travelled foreign correspondent. I was yet to learn that proper travellers don't festoon their luggage with labels announcing where they've been (they have much more subtle ways of doing that – see *Vanity Cases*).

But once you start to trot the globe you begin to realise what a very large globe your earthshrinker exercises are trying to encompass. The more places I got to, the more places it seemed I hadn't been to.

One of these blanks on my map was the United States, the first foreign land I had ever longed to visit as a globestruck boy. Not, as you might assume, because my imagination was fired by cowboy and gangster films and shots of Harold Lloyd clinging to the flagpoles of skyscrapers. I was seized with a burning desire to cross the Atlantic from the moment when, at the age of ten or eleven, there fell into my hands an American comic book containing a mouth-watering advertisement for a caramelised confection known as Turtles, so called because they were fashioned in the shape and size of terrapins. To one confined to a diet of aniseed balls and sherbet dabs –

and even these were in short supply with wartime sweet rationing – these exotic boxed candies were as a mirage. I yearned to go to America and stuff myself with Turtles.

The opportunity was not to come until I had lost my sweet tooth. The stiff currency exchange controls still in force twelve years after the war, which made it impossible for anyone to visit the United States under his own steam, were relaxed slightly to allow travellers £100-worth of currency per foreign trip. This made it just possible for ordinary tourists to take an American holiday for the first time since the autumn of 1939. I persuaded my newspaper to give me a hundred pounds in dollars (then 2.80 to the pound) and let me see how far it would take me.

Launching myself from a fifteen-dollar-a-night fleapit hotel off Times Square, I got as far as Miami Beach and back by Greyhound – 3,000 miles through nine states at eight old pence a mile – before the money ran out, sometimes putting up in boarding houses, sometimes snatching a few hours' sleep on the bus as it rolled southwards through the night. Philadelphia, Baltimore, Washington DC, Richmond, Newport News, Raleigh, Charleston, Savannah, Jacksonville . . . I thrill to the Greyhound depot Tannoy's sonorous roll-call even now, remembering how it sirened me on from one state to the next – to see what lay around the corner. I had an open ticket that allowed me to stop off at any place that took my fancy, catching the next bus out after I had exhausted the possibilities of Atlantic City's boardwalk or seen all I could of the City of Brotherly Love before the urge to move on tugged me away. The self-conducted Greyhound tour – in the fullness of time I was to cover most of the country from coast to coast and border to border by this means – remains for me the best and cheapest way of seeing the United States (see *Ways and Means*). But I never did get to taste those Turtles. Though I spotted them often enough in Main Street candy store windows, they didn't tempt me any more. I had another appetite now.

Within a fortnight of saying goodbye to Broadway I was in Moscow, at the start of a six-week, 8,000-mile tour that was to take me as far as Samarkand on Marco Polo's silk road to China. I was invited to a Ukrainian wedding in Sochi, got drunk with the labelling department foreman of a champagne factory in Georgia, and encountered a beetle as big as a mouse in my bedroom in Alma-Ata. At last I was entitled to call myself a travelling man of sorts.

But while I have ever since clocked up at least 25,000 miles a year, my globetrotting claims remain modest. There are businessmen who cover more ground in a year than I do in a decade (though a conference suite in Bangkok is much the same as a conference suite in Brussels). Jet-hopping journalists travel tremendous distances, but mostly they see only what they have come to see, file their story, and take the next plane out. (I remember sharing a sundowner on a Cairo hotel balcony with a press photographer who stubbornly refused to turn round and take in a breathtaking view of the Pyramids, since they held no interest for him unless Princess Diana happened to be standing in front of them.) I like to stand and stare. I have stared longer at some places than at others. California asked me to stay and I did, for several months. South Africa asked me to leave and I haven't been back since. I am more at home in towns and cities than in the wide open spaces, and beaches bore me: I must be the only person who has ever spent two weeks in Sydney without ever setting foot on Bondi Beach. I am positively not intrepid. Not since I walked all the rivers in Yorkshire from source to mouth as a young man (because they were there) have I ventured into that backpack-and-anorak area where travelling leaves off and mountaineering begins. I like to travel in comfort, if not in style. And I do like a roof over my head at night.

But otherwise my requirements are as modest as my credentials. While I am as avid as the next tourist for my first glimpse of Niagara Falls or the Acropolis, I am as happy in a humdrum commercial town as in the capital city with its museums and monuments or the famous resort with the azure sea below it and the snow-capped mountains behind. It is, as I said, the very foreignness of foreign places which captivates me – the characteristic smells (New York smells of Danish pastry, Athens of sweet coffee, Venice of drains, the entire Middle East of barbecued kid), the unfamiliar neon signs with their upside-down exclamation marks, the cars parked on the pavement, the dusty palm trees, the boulevards, the bazaars, the way the shopkeepers have of wrapping your toothpaste in paper and string instead of slinging it into a paper bag. I want everything to look different from its equivalent at home: blood-red stucco or clapboard instead of brick, domes instead of spires, banknotes like lottery tickets, triangular stamps, peasant women wearing clogs, ashtrays advertising Pernod, dogs with muzzles, shuttered windows, flat sugar lumps, men standing at zinc bars with camel-hair overcoats draped across their shoulders. I want to (and did) see real cowboys in Laramie, camel trains in the Sahara, kangaroos in the outback (but I couldn't find Spaghetti Bolognese in Bologna). Nothing must even sound like home: the church bells must ring out louder and longer and at a different pitch, the car horns must parp-parp in that particularly continental way of theirs, the rolling stock on the Atcheson, Topeka and Santa Fe railroad must sound that mournful two-tone whistle we remember from old Westerns (and it does). I want to be in a different time zone. I don't want anything looking or sounding English (though I do rather draw the line at the rather panto-sounding Peking suddenly becoming Beijing in travel literature – the geographical equivalent of metrication). In New Zealand I changed my hotel bedroom because the view from my window looked too much like the Sussex Downs. They gave me a room overlooking a back alley of ramshackle wooden workshops with verandahs and corrugated iron canopies. That suited me fine. I was palpably abroad.

(This wanting foreign places to look foreign cuts both ways. I am told that what most disappoints the Japanese about our country is that we don't all wear bowler hats and carry furled umbrellas.)

There are those (see *Those Who Don't*) who detest abroad, for whom travel narrows the mind, who like

Miss Mitford's Uncle Matthew fulminate against its unutterable bloodiness. This little book is patently not for them. Conversely, there are those who are more at home abroad than in their native land, and it is not for them either. It is for those who have travelled a bit and aspire to travel more, but not up Mount Everest (though tourist litter is now a problem at the Everest Base Camp). But just as its companion volume *The Theory & Practice of Lunch* is not a good food guide, neither is this a travel guide. I make no recommendations as to where you might go or how you should get there. But if you are contemplating setting off somewhere – and who is not, all the year round, whether they will ultimately get there or not? – then *The Theory & Practice of Travel* should oil the wheels.

> *They spell it Vinci and pronounce it Vinchy;*
> *foreigners always spell better than they*
> *pronounce.*

> MARK TWAIN

What Is Travel For?

There are those who believe that travel has never been the same since Thomas Cook, in promoting a railway excursion to a temperance meeting in Lough-borough in 1841, invented the day tripper. Certainly it was thereabouts that travellers, like the railways themselves, began to separate themselves into three classes: I am a traveller, you are a tourist, he is a tripper.

The tripper element need not detain us long. No longer temperance and no longer curfewed into get-ting there and back in a single day, they roam the world, vomiting on the ferries, tossing their fizzy drink cans into the lily pools of the Taj Mahal, paint-ing the toenails of the copy of Michelangelo's David in the Piazza della Signoria. Why do philistines bother to go to Florence, vandals to Venice, when they could spend their money on video nasties and just stay at home? They are the soccer louts of tourism, a roaring nuisance even when doing no active physical damage beyond polluting the atmosphere. The underclass of the age of affluence, trippers, like the poor, are always with us. The most we can hope for is that our paths do not cross.

Tourists do at least mean well, even the fabled American who told his wife to do the inside of Westminster Abbey while he did the outside. They go to Florence to be able to say they have seen the treasures of the Medici, not to urinate in the Neptune Fountain. The trouble is that a million pairs of feet a year are tramping across the priceless mosaic floors of the Uffizi Gallery. Venice gets so crowded that the Eurocoaches are turned back on the causeway. Tourists are the locusts of travel, devouring culture and crisps in more or less equal proportions, creating a trillion-dollar industry but gradually destroying all that stands before them.

Who, then, are the travellers? Largely, these days, they are figments of their own imagination – that's discounting explorers and bona fide backpackers on walking tours of the Himalayas. Travellers see themselves on the Channel packet with the briar pulling nicely and a dog-eared *Baedeker* in the patch pocket of their tweeds. The reality is that they are as likely as not to be found cooling their heels at Gatwick or Heathrow, just like everybody else in search of sun or snow. Travellers are, indeed, tourists – but, if one can say it without snobbery, with a better brand image. For one thing, they do not add to the burden of the tourist season: you do not find them mopping their brows in Pompeii in high summer. Nor do they hunt in packs, much less in packages.

Furthermore, they are tourists in the most literal sense in that they do tour – they do not stay put. Whither the traveller goeth, it is not long before he goeth somewhere else, a glutton for side trips and excursions and a perpetual seeker after greener grass. And travellers are trailblazers. Where they go, others follow. Many of the resorts that are now tourist clichés were unspoiled backwaters when first stumbled upon by travellers, who unfortunately could not resist telling the folks back home about them. As Europe fills up and the marble steps wear out, travellers tend to strike out farther and farther: Thailand, Burma, Brazil, Malaysia. But the truth is that they are not, now, usually innovators: these outposts of the tourist empire have been set up for them by enterprising tour operators who in turn have been lured by the burgeoning hotel industry in faraway places.

And why not? Travellers do not want to sleep in tents and wash in streams any more; their pioneering instinct is channelled into checking out the coffee shop of the Xanadu Hyatt Regency for the hordes who will follow. 'Go to Turkey before the blight of tourism sets in,' advises a newspaper travel writer, thus bringing the blight nearer. But of course, when Turkey is spoiled for the traveller, he will no longer be going there. He will be in Tibet. So where the tripper is a lout and the tourist is a locust, the traveller is, it has to be said, a benevolent parasite like ivy, enhancing the host structure (or anyway the host's pocket) but inevitably weakening the fabric. No wonder – to get the quotation out of the way – Robert Louis Stevenson said that to travel hopefully was a better thing than to arrive.

What, then, is to be said for the traveller? What is he about? What is his travelling for? The answer would seem to be that he is a civilising influence – upon himself, if no longer very much on others.

Travel does indeed broaden the mind. You approach a new country as you open a new book – something has to be gleaned from it, only superficially perhaps, but then most casual learning is superficial. Reading Elizabeth David's *French Provincial Cooking* does not make me a cook or teach me how to become one, but it does inform me on the subject. A trip to Brittany or the Périgord does not qualify me to become a guide to these provinces nor does it fit me to answer a travel quiz about them, but it does enlighten me a little. The country I know best outside my own is the United States – and all I know for sure after a hundred visits and perhaps a total of two years of my life spent there is that I do not know it at all. But I know some things about it.

Travel feeds one of the most basic of all animal instincts, which is curiosity. Even a cow, which is not very bright, will trouble to lumber the length of a field simply to look over a wall. There is not a shoreline in the world, however hostile, that some mariner has not headed for at whatever risk to life and limb, to see what it encompasses. The traveller, however pampered, always has the itch to move on – even though he may make it a condition that there is a dry martini available at journey's end.

Travel puts serendipity in motion. The art of making happy discoveries by chance is not entirely accidental: the voyager has to set off in the first place. The traveller it is who finds the out-of-the-way village where the smell of garlic-tinged sauces leads him to the one little bistro where the last vacant table is enticingly laid with bread, oil, lemons, a bowl of shiny black olives, and rough wine. But however idyllic and tranquil the setting, however secluded the sandy cove and bustling the market place, however cheap, however unspoiled, it is not the traveller who returns year after year after year. The traveller may be on holiday but he does not go on holiday for rest and contentment – well, not entirely. The village is pretty, yes, a find, yes – but what's the next village like?

Travel is experience. It engages all the five senses. While we may have agreed that the traveller is only a tourist in a white linen suit and a panama hat, here is another difference between them: where the tourist only tastes, the traveller savours. He wants to try all the local dishes, he will drink nothing but the local wine. He will have a stab at speaking the language, and even if he can't master a word of it will prefer to be among the natives than among his own nationality. The Olde Englishe Pubbe, run by a bare-kneed couple from Dagenham, knows him not – indeed, if the resort boasts such an establishment he is unlikely to be there in the first place (though he does not write off Spain because of the Costa del Disco). He avoids tourist traps, even gently ensnaring ones where a boutique selling tat that could be bought in Oxford Street is disguised as the chandler's store or native bazaar or peasant craft shop.

Above all, the traveller finds the time – makes the time – to stand and stare. At the Louvre, the tourist makes straight for the Mona Lisa, gawps, buys a picture postcard of it, and repairs to the nearest croissanterie, or worse, the nearest McDonald's. The traveller takes in all the galleries he can digest at one go, then reaps the reward of the virtuous with a slap-up lunch at a Michelin-rated bistro.

The more we look at it, the more it is apparent that there is one more comparison to be made between the traveller and the tourist. The traveller has by far the better time. Tourism is exhaustion with little to show for it. Travel is enjoyment with much to remember. That is what it is for.

Armchair Travelling

Ideally there should be a Sherlock Holmes fog without and Billy Bunter muffins within. There should be an atmosphere of leather armchairs and warmly glowing lamps, and the floor should be littered with maps, guides and brochures.

It is the perfect way to travel. No airport hassle, no jet lag, no shuffling queue through immigration, no anxious wait by the carousel. And the beauty of it is that if you grow tired of the Côte d'Azur or become bored with Yugoslavia, you can be in Rio or New South Wales at the turn of a page.

But having got yourself thoroughly in the mood for going places, you must sooner or later (there's no hurry – or if there is, you've let the armchair travelling season slip through your fingers) get down to the practicalities.

Four questions have to be answered, with much cross-referring back and forth. Where do you want to go? Why do you want to go? When do you want to go? How do you want to go?

Let us consider the where and the why in tandem. You have clipped and filed (haven't you?) all those

The floor should be littered with maps, guides and brochures

travel pieces with headings like 'Take A Break In Tibet' and 'Away From It All In Alaska' which these days grace the Sunday and weekend papers all year round. Or anyway, such of them as caught your fancy and are within your budget. While the trips that yield these reports may be funded or subsidised by the tourist industry, so that the likelihood of coming across the headline 'Benidorm Is Bloody Awful' is slim, they are usually far more impartial and certainly far more informative than common or garden brochures, which you need only consult after drawing up a short list of possibles (and not before you have turned to *How to Speak Brochurese*).

So let the pendulum swing wildly for a while, between one country and another, one continent and another, one culture and another, between the teeming Khan al Khalili with its gold beaters and carpet sellers and their Mother Courage entourage of itinerant bootblacks, barbers, beggars, olive-vendors, tea-carriers, money-changers and renters-out of bubble pipes, and camera-clicking Fisherman's Wharf with its souvenir T-shirts and sour-dough bread and crabs and lobsters and conch shells and candy floss. Before giving the pendulum the chance to settle, you should be asking yourself why you want to go wherever you'll be going. What do you want from this trip? Do you just want to recharge your batteries, eat a few good meals and come back relaxed? Then Cairo is out. Or do you have an urge to get right off the beaten track this time, to see the unfamiliar, to find some spot at the back of beyond where no one at the office or golf club has ever set foot? Then San Francisco is out too.

But do keep it at the back of your mind that when Montaigne said that all permanent decisions are made in a temporary frame of mind, he could have been talking about going along to the travel agent's and plonking down a deposit. You may yearn for sun and sea now, when you've just finished lagging the cistern, but how are you going to feel in May when there is an invigorating bustle in the air and the city boulevards and piazzas beckon? Or if you're hankering to see Petra, the rose-red city half as old as time, is it going to start niggling away at you that you who have never ridden so much as a seaside donkey have committed yourself to a journey that can only be completed on horseback?

It's a matter of consulting your temperament. Do you really like solitude, or only in the abstract? Do crowds faze you, or do you rather like being part of a throng? If the latter, how much of a throng can you put up with? Would it bother you to arrive in Bali only to discover that it has become the Australians' Benidorm? Or to alight on a North American Indian reservation to find the main attraction is a bingo hall? Which – and be honest – is your priority: ticking off the sights, or lingering in a good restaurant (once out of Europe, they do not necessarily go hand in hand)? In short: your choice of holiday venue may make you feel adventurous or virtuous – but will your temperament enjoy itself?

The next question is, when do you propose the

expedition should take place? Mad dogs and Englishmen not only go out in the midday sun, they go to Sorrento in August. Again it is a matter of temperament. If you must join the annual migration to the Med, where in Sir David Attenborough's memorable phrase, 'humans spend their time on strips of sand beside the sea where they lie as thickly as seals on breeding beaches', then you must. But is your temperament a martyr to sunburn? How are you on humidity? How would you take to Hong Kong in June when the rainfall is twice the average for an Amazonian rain forest? Before making any final decisions, check out the weather tables for the month in which you will be travelling. Consider the seething horde count too: you may be able to tolerate your fellow human beings in great quantity in the cool breeze of spring, but could it become something of a strain when the thermometer is hitting ninety and they are still teeming in? Have another word with your temperament, and should it have any reservations, think again.

As to how you are going to get there, this question is as often as not decided for you (unless, not a bad way of doing it, you decide on your mode of travel first and then find out where it can get you). You cannot, after all, get to the Canary Islands by tram. Where there is a choice of transport, however, and you are not locked into a flying package, then the period allowed for armchair travelling should be doubled to accommodate a leisurely browse through *Cook's International Timetable* to see whether it is, then, possible to get to the Canary Islands by train and ferry. (It is. Catch the London–Marseilles train at Victoria, then take the Adriatica Line.) But these weighty matters are looked at in a separate section. See *Ways and Means*.

Much armchair travelling is in the realm of pipe-dreams – so much so that when you finally do make a choice it can be a bit of a letdown. Paris may seem a bit tame when Peru, however peripherally, has been on the list of possibilities. Never mind: there is always next time, and once you have got down your Paris *Michelin* and started sketching out an itinerary that deposits you each lunchtime on the doorstep of a crossed-knives-and-forks bistro or brasserie, Peru will recede into the atlas to become once again a far-off country about which you wish to know little.

Yet, dismissing the pipedream territories, have you made the best choice? Well, in the first place, you are under no obligation to buy simply because you have squeezed the fruit. You may be planning your holiday months ahead but there is no reason why you should sign on the dotted line for it months ahead, much though your travel agent would like you to. So you have plenty of time to change your mind. And notwithstanding any inducements the tour operators may offer to tempt you into booking early, by holding out until a few weeks before take-off you could get a bargain among the discount holidays then on offer. A risk, perhaps, but if you can't get where you wanted to be, there's always somewhere else. Peru, perhaps. Back to the old armchair planning.

But even if you do finish up making what turns out to be the wrong choice, does it matter all that much? It would certainly have mattered a great deal at one time, when one holiday a year was the norm, and if it rained every day then the holiday was a washout and a write-off to be brooded over for the next twelve months; but in these more flexible and flusher days, when it's nothing out of the ordinary to take four, five, even six breaks in a year, one dud holiday is not the end of the world. Besides, who says it is going to be a dud? Your Shangri-La may not be as exotic as you'd hoped for when you get there, but it certainly will be by the time you start telling your traveller's tales about it.

*A good holiday is one spent among people
whose notions of time are vaguer than yours.*

J. B. PRIESTLEY

Good Companions

There are many groups of opposites in the travelling life – those who don't see the point of checking in until the last possible moment, and those who arrive early enough for the previous flight; those who have no sense of direction and those who can find their way through the Hampton Court Maze blindfold; those who want to go somewhere new and those who want to return to somewhere familiar; those who worship the sun and those who come out in a rash. And all these pairs are married to one another.

Like Jack and Mrs Spratt, travellers in a long-term relationship have to learn to accommodate one another. The fact that so many of them are still married is an indication that this is not asking the impossible – though it would be interesting to know how many divorces have stemmed from one partner remembering the air tickets while the other one has forgotten the passports.

One way of smoothing the path is to acknowledge that spending twenty-four hours a day, seven days a week, with even the most agreeable of companions is going to cause tension. Since at least one major quarrel is guaranteed, it is best got over early. A list of suitable things to quarrel about appears under *Useful Phrases*.

But indeed there is really no need to live in one another's pockets all the time. Travellers wise to one another's tolerance levels will make a point of spending an hour or so apart each day. A good time for one partner to clear off on some errand or other is while the other is having a bath and getting changed. Then again, if one of you likes churches and the other doesn't, there is nothing to be gained by the secular one traipsing around looking like a martyred saint. Better to do some shopping and arrange to meet up later. But, and without wishing to intrude into any-one's private life, parting company at bedtime is not generally a good idea. It is not the best of starts to the day when one partner is as fresh as paint while the other has been propping up the bar until three in the morning.

There should be strict demarcation on tasks and duties. One person and one person only should be responsible for all documentation. One person should be appointed timekeeper, with full responsibility if the flight is missed, or conversely if you wind up meandering round and round the duty-free shop for two and a half hours. One should be appointed cashier. And there can only be one map reader – usually the one with the better eyesight.

Again this may be on too personal a note, but I would keep domestic preoccupations at bay while on one's travels. Not only do they intrude where they have no business, but in exotic surroundings it is incongruous to allow oneself to be overheard discussing – as I overheard a couple wandering around Pompeii – the need to get the guttering fixed. I was reminded of the classic copulation joke, 'Sam, the bedroom ceiling needs painting.' I would extend the embargo to marital preoccupations, but the truth is that there's nothing like being a long way from home for fanning the flames. That's fine if they're amatory, second honeymoon flames – but usually they're not. As Andy Capp once perceptively observed, who did you ever know who went on a third honeymoon? Whatever smouldering resentments may be under the surface, this is the time they tend to erupt in bonfires. Hence the case for quarrelling early. But don't make it terminal.

If your choice of travelling companion isn't a Hobson's one, there are certain preoccupations you can take upfront to avoid the trip degenerating into a fiasco.

Never travel with anyone who holds conflicting views to yours about smoking, drinking, sunbathing, sightseeing, sex, shopping, punctuality, gregariousness, the importance of meals, the jollity of discos, the funniness of foreigners, or hygiene (personal and as regards washing lettuce). If the trip is self-catering, establish which self will be doing the catering.

Couples of the opposite sex travelling together who do not have a cohabitation policy should establish one before they set off. Should they decide on a platonic expedition (and such things have been known) then they should be clear, if only tacitly so, whether either party is regarded as at liberty to take up with a foreigner of the worst sort.

Women travelling as a twosome, and who don't know each other all that well, should agree in advance on the desirability or otherwise of chatting up ski instructors, beach boys or those nice blokes at the next table. There should also be rules of etiquette in the event that one finds herself infatuated while the other doesn't.

If you are a family travelling with another family, you should ideally have done it before and rated it a good idea; otherwise you should be well acquainted with one another's children and be able to put up with them, with scolding rights being mutually granted. Two couples plus offspring living on top of one another are twice as potentially explosive as one couple living on top of one another, so it is essential to get out of each other's way regularly, babysitting for one another in turn. On self-catering holidays – you will already have established that the other party is not addicted to making eel stew or playing the piano – the men of the group should not suffer from the delusion that the women are happy shopping, cooking and nattering together while they explore the bars. The worst thing one couple can say to the other is 'Can't you keep your children quiet?' The worst thing one partner can say to the other is 'Can't you keep your children quiet?' This is almost equalled by 'Why not leave the cooking to Annabel, darling, she's so much better at it?'

If you're one childless (or child-unburdened) couple travelling with another, ask yourselves in all earnestness, before signing anything, whether there is the remotest chance of the following well-known phrase or saying cropping up in private conversation before the holiday is over:

'They're your bloody friends, darling – you would insist on coming away with them.'

How to Speak Brochurese

The key to all holiday brochures is the picture of the hotel swimming-pool. What you see is it. There isn't any more. Although the water laps the edge of the photograph to give you the impression that there's twice as much pool if only they had the space to show it, a millimetre more and you would see dry land. That peculiar triangle shape is not a segment of a huge Olympic-sized pool. It is a complete, close-cropped representation of a peculiarly triangular-shaped pool.

The same goes for bedrooms, where the photograph likewise contrives to suggest that there is a lot more room to the east of the twin beds. There isn't. When the photographer took that picture, it was with his back pressed up against the wall, or inside the wardrobe if that is not shown.

The bird's eye view of the beach looks inviting. The reason it's a bird's eye view is that shooting from a few feet back on the hotel roof, the camera avoids the four-lane highway that your balcony overlooks.

But anyone booking a holiday solely on the recommendation of a brochure, particularly a tour operator's brochure, must be suffering from anticipatory heatstroke. The only real use of a brochure, apart from giving you a vague idea what a resort looks like with the abattoir obliterated (that's why the picture is L-shaped) is to convey the only solid information it contains, which is the price. This is the one area in which the brochure cannot lie – or anyway, not much. A hundred metres in brochurese may mean half a mile, and two mins may mean ten mins, but £246 for fourteen days means £246 for fourteen days – plus, of course, the fuel surcharge you may be asked for even though the strength of the pound against the dollar has brought fuel prices down.

To find out what the place is really like, consult a guide book, which as well as mentioning the prominence of the abattoir will probably also list the hotels, with a no-frills summary of their amenities and a clear indication of their position on, or off, the town map. If this information is too skimpy, consult a hotel guide for the region if there is one, and if there isn't, talk to your travel agent. Some holiday specialists, notably Hogg Robinson and Lunn Poly, put out their own hotel guides which, while not quite in the same class for frankness as the old Roy Brooks house ads ('Second bedroom, suit dwarf but no cat-swingers please') are engagingly impartial. Other agents have their own under-the-counter guide books and in response to direct questions, such as 'Look, does "within easy reach of airport" mean it's built on the edge of the runway or not?', they may give you a direct answer. If they give you an evasive one ('The only other information we have is that it has unobstructed views of the distant mountains'), there is something to hide.

You may, at the end of the day, be driven back to the brochure: in which case it is as well to have a smattering of brochurese. A Concise Dictionary of Brochurese follows:

ALL WITH BATH OR SHOWER – yours is with shower.

AMENITIES – noun used to make what is singular sound plural, e.g., shopping amenities = shop.

BRAND-NEW COMPLEX – unfinished.

BUFFET-STYLE – queues.

BUSTLING HOTEL IN ONE OF THE LIVELIEST AREAS – conga line under your window at 3 a.m.

CLOSE TO NIGHTLIFE (OR NITELIFE) – over disco.

COLOURFUL – fruit and veg.

COMMANDING VIEWS – up a steep hill.

COMPLIMENTARY COCKTAIL ON ARRIVAL – ill-printed voucher on arrival, which may be exchanged in bar for foul green drink.

COURTESY COACH TO POINTS OF INTEREST – out in the sticks, no buses.

EXTENSIVELY RENOVATED – concrete mixer on sun-deck.

FACILITIES – do-it-yourself, as in tea-making
facilities (no room service), drying facilities (no
laundry), conference facilities (underground
room with slide projector).
FEW (as in few minutes from) – many.
FRIENDLY ATMOSPHERE – slack service.
GENTLE SLOPE – one-in-three gradient.
INFORMAL – bare chests at breakfast.
INTERNATIONAL CUISINE – melon boats.
JOLLY ATMOSPHERE – raucous.
JUST MINUTES AWAY – bus every half hour.
KING-SIZED (as in double bed) – no room for queen.
LIVELY – full of *Sun* readers.
MANY (as in many other attractions) – few.
MODERN – concrete egg-box.
MODERNISED – bedroom sliced up to
accommodate shower unit.
NO FRILLS – bring your own coathangers.
NOT THE RITZ – not even the Station Hotel.
OVERLOOKING – used strictly in the sense of
ignoring, hence overlooking sea means
overlooking railway lines in between.
QUIET LOCATION – in outer suburbs.
RELAXING MAÑANA STYLE – utter
incompetence.
REFURBISHED – lowered ceiling, concealed
lighting.
SECLUDED – round a corner.
SIMPLY FURNISHED – plywood fittings.
SPECTACULAR SCENERY – half-way up a
mountain.
STRIKING – ugly.
SUN-DRENCHED – hot.
THRIVING – overcrowded.
TWO MAGNIFICENT POOLS – two small pools,
one of them drained.

VALUE FOR MONEY – read small print.

VIRTUALLY ON EXCELLENT SANDY BEACH –
across road from building blocking view of
excellent sandy beach.

WILL BE PART OF THE AMENITIES – not yet built.

WITHIN WALKING DISTANCE – cab-ride.

1 brochure metre	= 3 metres
1 brochure minute	= 5 minutes
1 brochure person (as in 'sleeps six')	
	= 1 half-person

Complimentary cocktail on arrival

Maps & Guides

On the wall behind my desk is mounted a handsome brass and wire mesh luggage rack, formerly the property of the Great Western Railway. It is piled high with maps. Wherever I venture, and no matter how brief my stay, I immediately buy a street map. Creased and tattered, dog-eared, patched with Sellotape, asterisked with the locations of restaurants and post offices, annotated with scribbled addresses, my maps are a more graphic *aide-mémoire* than any snapshot of the places I have been to. Picking out a clutch at random, I am transported at once to Old Jerusalem, to Helsinki, to Johannesburg, and now to Windsor, Ontario, where I only went for Sunday lunch on a side trip from Detroit across the river. (I remember calling the telephone operator to ask if Canada was open on Sundays. 'Why yes, sir,' he replied courteously. 'Canada is open all year round.') When I am too old and doddery to face the rigours of Heathrow any longer, my maps will do the travelling for me.

There are maps and maps. My map of Los Angeles, which tries to swallow the entire 64-square-mile conurbation in one gulp, is virtually useless except as a picnic tablecloth. Nowadays I use a set of interconnecting neighbourhood maps. On the other hand, I have a huge map of Cairo which shows every tiny souk and back alley as clear as day, the only confusing element being that they all seem to have the same name.

I notice that the street names on some of my older maps are in smaller type than I thought when I bought them. Eyesight is the only sensible criterion for settling on the scale of a map: better an unwieldy map you can read than a compact one which is just a blur. Pick one with a comprehensive street index and generous table of features of interest. Don't ever buy a map without opening it out: unless you are interested in cemeteries and golf courses (which reminds me – I have a very good map of Woodlawn Cemetery, NY, in my collection), you will not want to know about the outer suburbs, which do tend to be included in very many city maps. If you need a road map for driving, make sure it's an up-to-date one showing the new by-pass and the motorway extension. Street maps don't date so easily – unlike our own dear built-up areas, foreign towns do not usually bulldoze themselves out of recognition every few years.

There is more to using a map than identifying the thoroughfare you want to be on. You also have to be going the right way. If the Rue du 15 Octobre is on the left of the Boulevard du 8 Juillet on your map but on the right in actuality, either the map is upside down or you are, or you are facing the wrong way. Be sure to fold it back into its natural creases, otherwise it will tear. It will tear anyway with sufficient use, and the tear will be along the length of a street you have been trying to locate for half an hour. Finally, before we end these brief cartographical notes, I have a request from most of the population of Europe: please do not stand in the middle of their narrow pavements to pore over your map, as this drives passers-by into the gutter and under the wheels of crazed foreign drivers.

Maps should be bought on the spot; guide books should not, otherwise you are going to finish up with an overpriced, badly proof-edited fat volume printed on thick shiny paper and conveying more information than you can possibly need in impenetrable English ('On the left is the equestrian monument by Giambologna, who sculptured with a recalling spirit classic motives in the pedestal representing important matters'). Besides, as I urge elsewhere, guides should be part of your homework. It is rather an impertinence to arrive in a place not knowing the first thing about it. I recall being buttonholed in Rome by an American couple who wanted to know how to get to the Colosseum. I directed them as best as I could. Then they asked where they would find the Vatican, and I pointed them at the Metro. When they touched on the whereabouts of the Parthenon, sooner than put them to the embarrassment of learning that they were in the wrong capital of the wrong country for that, I thought it more tactful to suggest that they pick up a guide book. 'Where would we buy a guide book?' they asked.

We must not confuse guide books with travel books. Travel books describe journeys, impressions and experiences that will not necessarily be emulated by the reader, who is often, indeed, but an armchair traveller in the fullest sense who never goes further than Bognor Regis. Guide books are practical hand-books to be boned up on, annotated and packed in one's luggage.

Yet having said that, the best guide book I know is a travel book. This is James (Jan) Morris's *Venice*, which so absorbs and informs and rewards the reader, so swirls him up in the shimmering heat-mist of the lagoon, that to devour it before embarking on a trip to Venice is like having an extra week's holiday thrown in. On top of which, it is so much the epitome of what a travel book should be that I would recommend it even if you were going to Timbuktu, for it shows you how to open your eyes and look.

And one of the best travel books I know happens to be a guide book. This is *Reed's Nautical Almanac*, the bible for all who mess about in boats. Merely to open this chunky volume, with its tide tables and sea traffic routes and star charts and lists of lights, buoys and fog signals, and its Important General Notices to Mariners (*'Lizard Signal Station has now been discontinued as a maritime commercial signal station for Lloyd's, London'*) is to taste the salt tang of the sea. I cannot even look at *Reed's* without experiencing a severe case of wanderlust.

But what the more landlocked of us require is a practical guide to the spot we are about to visit. To start making recommendations in this area would take a book in itself. Nor is it an easy field. While there are many one-off guides to individual places, they are often too eccentrically non-comprehensive for the general traveller. Many of the more practical guides come in series. But which of them are any good? By way of taking soundings, try leafing through the guide to somewhere you happen to be familiar with. If it's a dud – skimpy, inaccurate, misleading, out of date – then you may bank on it that the rest in the series will be duds too.

For myself, I would always take the green *Michelin*, if there was one for the region, or one of the expanding series of American Express pocket guides which are compact, comprehensive and reliable. But at the end of the day, or the beginning of the trip, it all depends what you want a guide *to*. Some guides stick austerely to ruins and monuments, others lean more towards the nightlife and fleshpots. Then again, by consulting *Morocco On Ninepence A Day*, you are going to see a somewhat different Morocco from that conjured up by Berlitz. Incidentally, if the best guide available is to a whole region rather than the particular bit you're visiting, it saves carting the thing around with you if you photostat the relevant pages. NB: Take no notice of the prices quoted in any guide book. Like food guides, they always underestimate.

Travel books consulted for background briefing may be borrowed from the public library, but it is essential that guides should be bought and accompany you on your journey, later to take their place on a gradually expanding guide book shelf where, like my map collection, they may be browsed through in the long winter evenings to transport you back to that particular cool courtyard restaurant with the sunshine filtering through the hanging vines.

For the serious, inveterate, recidivist traveller, *The Traveller's Handbook* published by Heinemann with Wexas Ltd is essential. Packed with down-to-earth information on visas, vaccination requirements, airport taxes, shopping hours in Afghanistan and how not to get mugged in Bogotá (carry a machete), it also has the bonus of being printed on very thin paper which can be put to an alternative use in an emergency.

John Bull, like the snail, loves to carry his native shell with him, irrespective of changes of climate or habits of different conditions and necessities.

RICHARD FORD
A Handbook for Travellers in Spain 1855

Those Who Don't

Xenophobe was the Greek god who found it too humid up Mount Olympus, couldn't be doing with the sickly taste of nectar, and didn't see what was wrong with a good home-produced sacrifice instead of all that imported rubbish. Insular Athenians worshipped him – but from afar, since they didn't like to travel.

It remains a mystery how latter-day homebodies came to allow themselves to be tagged with such a funny foreign label, though. Perhaps the alternative to polysyllabic Greek was something disgustingly guttural in German. So xenophobes they are.

Like Gaul, a place they would advise us to take our own bottled water to should we have cause to visit it, xenophobes are divided into three parts, or rather three categories.

First there are those who loathe and abominate Abroad without qualification, or anyway profess to do so, never failing to give it the Komic Kapital endowed by their patron, Nancy Mitford's Uncle Matthew. Where their dislike is actual and not just a bit of real-ale posturing, the truth is that it is not only foreigners they cannot stand at any price, it is just about everybody. The reason they do not go abroad is that on disgusting Frog beach or in revolting Frog bar they are likely to encounter more of this just-about-everybody class than in, say, the remoter village inns of Exmoor. So they are not so much xenophobes as misanthropes.

Then there are those who genuinely and literally cannot stomach foreign parts. Abroad makes them ill. It brings them out in a rash. It plays havoc with their alimentary tracts. Arriving thankfully back to the sanctuary of Dunroamin they speak feelingly of food that was 'swimming in oil', which to their delicate systems is as if it had been covered in axle-grease. If there is a tummy bug around, they get it. If there is sunstroke around, they get that too. Foreign travel affects their health and they should be excused it as servicemen with bunions used to be excused boots, with a special chit which they could carry as their anti-passport.

There are several sub-categories such as the never-agains (beach was polluted, plumbing didn't work, place was full of Germans) and the never-befores (nearly got run over, couldn't understand what they were jabbering about, didn't like all this tipping business), but we are not going to make converts there either. Let us pass on to the third class of xenophobes, for whom there is hope yet.

They have been abroad often, and indeed they persist in doing it. With certain unfavourite exceptions, such as once-enchanting Amsterdam which seems hellbent on turning itself into the Earls Court of Europe, they actually like foreign parts. They like the food. They like the wine. They like the weather, the cobbles, the garlicky smells. It is the company they do not take to. They believe that foreign parts are too good to waste on foreigners.

They would concede that arrogant Frenchmen have every right to barge around their own cafés with their coats draped over their shoulders, shaking hands with all and sundry, kissing one another on both cheeks, shrugging in Gallic manner and generally making an exhibition of themselves. But wouldn't it be nice if *Les Deux Magots* were in Kingston-upon-Thames? And yes, Italians little better than Venetians are fully entitled to disport themselves around St Mark's Square – but how much more seemly if the Grand Canal flowed through the Wirral.

But so long as they don't jabber too excitedly, wave their arms about overmuch, slap their lederhosen, click their heels or stuff themselves with their own weight in cream cakes, it's not so much those foreigners who are indigenous to the foreign country they are visiting that xenophobes of this type object to – the Swiss in Switzerland and the Swedes in Sweden are two fairly harmless examples that come to mind – as those they regard as doubly foreign, for instance Germans in Italy or Italians in Germany.

To find Brussels full of Belgians they regard as quite acceptable, since many Belgians do happen to live there and somebody has to serve the drinks. But for them to turn into the Grand' Place for a quiet coffee and find the whole square seething and bubbling like a great boiling custard with four coachloads of midwestern agricultural students all wearing yellow backpacks and taking photographs of one another at the tops of their voices, is to wish that crossing from one country to another were still as giant a leap for mankind as landing on the moon – which one of these days, they predict darkly, will be jam-packed with Japanese tourists.

And at this stage, since we are all nodding in agreement, let us admit that inside every traveller is a xenophobe trying to get back home, and press on.

Aeroplanes have added nothing to our enjoyment of height. The human eye still receives the most intense images when the observer's feet are planted on the ground.

EVELYN WAUGH

GETTING
THERE

Ways and Means

By Land . . .

Had I but world enough and time I should travel everywhere by train – but another condition is that the year would have to be no later than 1938.

Not that it is no longer possible to travel by rail in comfort. The last time I went to Amsterdam by train, I was so settled and contented that I was tempted to stay on board until it reached Moscow. British Rail's inter-city service, despite an inferiority complex that prompts them to try to pass themselves off as an airline with 'Cuisine 2000' food trays and such nonsenses, is as good a way of getting from London to Bristol or Manchester as any I can think of. If I have to go from New York to Washington or vice versa it is on a Metroliner with a dry martini in my hand.

But travelling in comfort is not the same as travelling in style. Outside India, where there are still trains fit for a maharajah, and China, with 'soft class' (People's Republic Newspeak for first) carriages fit for an emperor, and aside from the faked-up Orient Express, travelling in style (and not only by rail) is a thing of the past. By Grand Central Station I sit down and weep at having arrived too late to cross America on the Twentieth Century Limited (though as a matter of fact that splendiferous train, such a star among rolling stock that they made a musical of it, started from Chicago). *Le Train Bleu* restaurant is still the pride of the Gare de Lyon, but *le Train Bleu* on wheels is but a shunting shadow of its former self. And oh, my Golden Arrow of yesteryear! The last time I went from Victoria to Paris by train the buffet car was closed.

But there clings to railways and railway stations, like steam-age soot, an aura of romance such as the airways have not known since Imperial flying-boats with wickerwork chairs taxied out onto the grass of Croydon Aerodrome, and which the shipping lines lost when they lost the *Queen Mary*. Even totally deserted station halls – like the Union Pacific cavern in Cheyenne, Wyoming, where the last Deadwood stagecoach stands in the forecourt and the indicator board reads 'Trains West Mon, Wed, Fri, Trains East Tues, Thurs, Sat' – have a siren lure; and the bustling ones, with their smocked porters and ticket collectors dressed like station-masters and yellow *Partenze* timetable sheets, positively incite you to buy a ticket for Salzburg or Zagreb and clamber aboard. Nowhere is more uncompromisingly foreign than a foreign railway station, nowhere more calculated to tempt the reckless traveller on across the next frontier. Some of our own main line terminals convey the same whiff of wanderlust. I never take the Brighton line from Victoria without a wistful glance at the boat trains departure board, nor pass through Blackfriars without remembering that you could once walk up to the ticket office and book through to Sebastopol.

My first rail trip abroad of any substance was on the night train to Munich, the Rhine Express from Liverpool Street. I was disappointed not to see anyone even remotely like a beautiful spy, but the Ruritanian policeman who worked his way along the train examining passports actually did click his heels and say, 'Your papers, *mein Herr*.' How thrilling to start the day in an Alfred Hitchcock movie. Breakfast in Rotterdam, a couple of beers as we glided through the Rhine Valley, lunch – anything from a plate of cheese to a jellied pig's head – in Bonn, tea and a lightly boiled egg in Stuttgart, and the train was still spotless. I shared a table with an antiquarian bookseller who was off to Heidelberg. He confided that he never travelled any other way: 'Why fiddle about with seatbelts and plastic trays of unspeakable braised beef and celery, when one can go straight to one's berth, get a good night's rest and wake up refreshed, ready to do business?'

But then he had to spend all the next day on the train, I pointed out. 'True. All the more time to complete one's crossword.'

I have been a devotee of European trains ever since. In fact I cannot keep off them. If I fly to Brussels, it is only to consult my *Cook's Continental*

Timetable (which I refuse to call by its new Eurocrat name of *Cook's European Timetable*) to see which train will get me to Paris or Luxembourg in time for lunch. Just to keep temptation well in my way, all the European railways offer bargain rover tickets, mostly available from the European Rail Travel Centre at Victoria.

But while I like to travel by train I would not claim to be a railway buff. I use the train to see the world. Some fanatics use the world to see the trains. For them, there are still epic journeys to be made on the Trans-Siberian Express, the Peking to Moscow Trans-Mongolian Express, the Ost-West Express – trips I have experienced only vicariously in the closely-packed pages of *Cook's International Timetable*, a mine of railway nuggets such as that the Trans-Australian to Perth leaves Adelaide at 12.30, change trains at Port Pirie. Now that's a rail journey I do mean to make one of these days.

The next time I cross the United States at ground level, however, it will not be by the notoriously unpunctual Amtrak but by Greyhound. If you fancy the idea of nodding off in a Californian orange grove and waking up in the Arizona desert, I recommend it as a remarkably cheap way of getting about. You buy a runaround pass from the Greyhound office in London (14–16 Cockspur Street, SW1Y 5BL) – seven days' unlimited travel for £65, fifteen days' for £95 at the time I write – and then America is your oyster. The beauty of the arrangement is that if you are on your way to Salt Lake City when you are suddenly seized by a deep yearning to be in Yellowstone National Park, all you have to do is get off at the next stop and catch another bus going in a different direction. The driver will have the swagger of John Wayne ('All righty, folks, let's go to San Diego') and your fellow-passengers, who use these Greyhounds as their local bus, will seem like refugees from the old Norman Rockwell covers on the *Saturday Evening Post*.

The other way to see America is by car, picking your self-drive up at one centre and dumping it at another. There, too, are some very economical deals to be had, but with a general 55 mph speed limit, strictly applied in many states, it takes an awful lot of driving to get from one side of Texas to the other, and while I am a glutton for what Americans call 'scenic attractions', it is a big country and as you drive through apparently endless vistas you do begin to wonder just how much more prairie or cottonfield or desert you can take.

But nothing I can say will put off those travellers who are umbilically attached to the wheel, as many Channel-crossers are in particular, so I will not attempt to cross swords with anyone who believes that abroad begins at Dover. I am sure that driving on and off ferries is great fun (though it wasn't for me when I had to back off the crowded Ardrossan–Isle of Arran ferry in a hired car and I couldn't find reverse gear), and I can see the attraction of being able to get right off the beaten track where the chances of some maniac cutting in by right of way from a side road may well be minimised, since it is a side road you are on already, but taking one cart-wheel track with another, I still prefer to let the train take the strain.

Ever since childhood, when I lived within earshot of the Boston and Maine, I have seldom heard a train go by and not wished I was on it.

PAUL THEROUX

. . . and Sea . . .

If I cannot go by rail then I'd like to go by water –
but again I should prefer to be spirited back in a
time capsule to a plushier age of mahogany cabins
and chandeliers and polished brass and paddle-
steamers.

Come to think of it, I have been up the Nile and
down the Mississippi by paddle-boat, and both experiences carried faint foghorn echoes of those great
stateroom days. I have made the *QE2* crossing only
once, when the sensation of stepping back into the
Thirties generated by the Jack Buchanan and Jessie
Matthews flavour of the Southampton Ocean Terminal – all mirrors and maple panelling and fluted
columns and rounded corners – lasted only as far as
the gangplank. Where the *Queen Mary* was a floating
Ritz and the *Queen Elizabeth* a floating Savoy, the *QE2*
is a floating Inn on the Park – comfortable without
being extravagant, luxurious without going over the
top. No marble baths or Tudor fireplaces, but decor
which is the visual equivalent of Musak, joshing
stewards and a DJ who twitters on about tomorrow's
activities over the ship's radio: 'Even if you're not

46

into flower arrangements, you ladies, go and see the wowy things they do with flowers.' It was thrilling to be tugged away to the strains of *Land of Hope and Glory*, but I was a mite miffed, on arrival at the other side of what they still call the Pond, to find that the Statue of Liberty does not rise from the sea like Venus on the half shell, her upraised right arm giving an outsize impression of Excalibur on the shimmering horizon. It turns out to be a geographical impossibility. The first distinguishable landmark, I have to record, is the water tower of the Coney Island amusement park.

I'm not sure whether cruises are within my brief, since it seems to me that cruises are not really a means of going somewhere, merely a roundabout way of coming back. In any case, I have never been tempted towards cruising, mainly because the average age of my fellow-passengers would have been around sixty. Now that I am approaching sixty myself, however, I see that the cruise lines have decided that they must aim for a younger class of customer. One cruise advertisement purportedly quotes a 22-year-old girl: *'From the start it was go, go, go. I fell in with a great bunch of people who all liked the same things as me, like snorkelling, playing tennis and so on. The nightlife was great too. We usually ended up in the Island Disco until goodness knows when . . .'* So I think I can still thankfully regard myself as disqualified.

In any case, should I wish to swan about the Mediterranean and its associated seas, I should regard myself as better advised taking the motor vessel Orient Express from Venice to Istanbul, a glorified car ferry. Ferries are not what they were, but some ferries are more what they were than others – the Scandinavian and Baltic lines, for example. My favourite is the Harwich–Esbjerg crossing, with a smorgasbord lunch on the Nyborg–Korsør train ferry as we approach Copenhagen. The Channel ferries are tolerable when not plagued by hooligans or school parties playing ghetto blasters and throwing up green Chartreuse, but nowadays are very much geared to the kind of passenger who likes to munch crisps and stare at videos rather than march briskly up and down the deck. On the other side, as well as the jolly steamers plying the lakes of Switzerland and Italy, all the great European rivers are busy with commercial traffic. There is no better way of arriving in a city than along its waterway. Why fly to Budapest, for instance, when you can fly to Vienna and chug to Budapest down the Danube?

. . . to make you feel like an alcoholic

. . . and Air

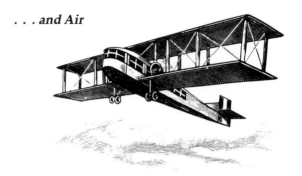

Which brings us, unless you have the inclination to get to Vienna by the alternative and more civilised means of the Arlberg Express, inexorably to the aeroplane.

The term used by the Royal Air Force for passengers is 'self-loading freight', and that just about sums up our status. The only thing to be said for flying is that it gets you where you want to be by the quickest means – though not as quick as the airlines would have us believe, when you take getting to and from airports and checking in and all the palaver at the other end into consideration. An undelayed trip to Washington by Concorde took me eight hours door to door (and it's a psychological oddity how the three-and-a-half-hour crossing in this rather cramped aircraft can seem like the conventional seven after all the hype about flying faster than sound).

Flight is so ubiquitous and commonplace that the person sitting next to you no longer feels obliged to strike up a conversation as if you were two explorers charting the same patch of the unknown. That is the only improvement I can think of in thirty-odd years of flying. Except for the pampered few in first class (and even there, standards and service have deteriorated) the food is terrible. The only decent meal I have ever had travelling economy was on a Bonanza Airways flight from San Francisco to Las Vegas, when they gave me a hamburger. Instead of keeping their meals basic and simple, airline caterers persist in fooling around with the food in the hope of passing it off as *haute cuisine*. They might just as well set out to provide an airborne bowling alley. In the realisation that no airline is ever going to get into the *Good Food Guide*, on European flights I never eat at all except to nibble the cold collation they sometimes give you. On long hauls I take sandwiches, which I eat under cover of darkness while everyone else is watching the movie.

It is becoming more and more difficult, especially on shorter flights, to get a drink. That's because the cabin staff have been instructed to push the duty-frees first. When they do finally start the drinks trolley going, it invariably sets off from the opposite end to where I am sitting. On the jumbos, where at least they start serving drinks from either end of the aisle, there is nothing like that long stretch of no-man's-land between two drinks trolleys moving at the speed of sludge to make you feel like an alcoholic. If you're really out of luck the service will be interrupted by turbulence, or abandoned altogether because they've spent so much time messing about that they've got to start serving up the food in order to get it cleared in good time to ask you to put out your reading light so everyone can watch a boring commercial for a hotel chain the airline happens to own.

What good things I can find to say about flying all seem to arise out of serendipity rather than the airline actually living up to its advertisements. Finding a flight half-empty is good. So is being bumped up to first class (though I always imagine, in my paranoiac way, that the cabin staff are treating me a shade less royally than their authentic first-class customers). A view of Manhattan or San Francisco Bay on a cloudless day is almost worth flying for. Sometimes there's a friendly stewardess who reminds me of the way stewardesses used to be, when passengers would ask them for their telephone numbers. Occasionally there's even a movie worth seeing.

But there's so much flight about that more must mean worse: there's a Gresham's Law to flying with the bad driving out the good. The really infuriating thing about bad airlines is that there's absolutely nothing to be done about them (complaining is like treading glue, and if you do it on the spot those Barbie Doll stewardesses can turn really nasty sometimes) except blackballing one in favour of another. But it appears to be a firm principle of air travel that the better an airline seems when you first switch over to it, the worse it will become as you continue to patronise it. Therefore the only advice I can offer as to flying, other than that Row 29 on a Boeing 747 gives you the most leg-room but against that it is next to the lavatories, is that given by *Punch* to those about to marry ('Don't'). But *Punch* reckoned without shot-gun weddings. Travellers fly because they have to, not because they want to.

Being bumped up to first class

Which Travel Agent?

Generalising about travel agents is like generalising about greengrocers or ironmongers or pork butchers or any other kind of shop. There are good corner shops and corner shops where they're always out of coffee and the cat's asleep on the bacon slicer; there are good supermarkets and supermarkets that hide the fresh produce behind the stuff with today's sell-by date, and which won't give you a free carrier bag; and then there are supermarket chains where one branch is staffed by gormless incompetents and another by as bright and helpful a bunch as you could wish for.

And there are ironmongers who don't sell butter and eggs – so as well as seeking a paragon among travel agents you are also looking for one who offers the range of services you require. (Of course, there is no obligation to put your butter and eggs in the same basket. Many travellers use different agents for different purposes.)

Given that you haven't gone to a bucket shop (and there are good and bad bucket shops too, by the way) and that your travel agent carries the sticker of the Association of British Travel Agents (ABTA), indicating that he is no end of a responsible chap with a professional code of conduct, it may be your assumption that you're automatically going to get good service. But the snag is, you're not going to be served by a travel agent, you're going to be served by a travel clerk.

Now your travel clerk may or may not yet have been on a training course, and if not could well belong to that very large group of young persons who leave school each year believing, for example, that Dublin is in the South China Sea and that the river that starts near the equator and supplies the Aswan Dam is the River Dee. (Those are actual examples from an Associated Examining Board survey, following complaints from travel agents that they are getting job applicants who don't know where anywhere is.)

Untrained clerks can be rich mines of misinformation (so can trained ones, come to that). I have been told, by chits of girls and spotty youths working for reputable agencies, that I can't buy a package to Florence at four days' notice without insuring against cancellation, that they're not allowed to issue an unreserved rail ticket to Newcastle unless I furnish them with my private telephone number, that only charter flights go to Nice, that there are no direct flights from London to Boston, and so on through a morass of mis-read timetables, ill-digested computer print-outs and half-understood regulations. The supervisor will sort out such misunderstandings, of course, but what you then have is a sullen clerk doing everything woodenly by the book.

And then, in this as in every other branch of the service industry, you get staff who just don't like the work, who roll their eyes and sigh when the client dithers between one resort and another, or who are otherwise offhand, lackadaisical, in a sulk with the boss or just plain stroppy.

Luckily there is no shortage of travel agencies, in fact there are more of them in the High Streets than shoe shops and building societies, so if you meet indifference or incompetence or unwillingness to call up alternative information on the computer screen (computer idleness is the bane of the business), it's easy enough to take your custom elsewhere. And while you're about it, compare prices. Competition has forced even the oldest-established travel agencies into some genteel bucket-shopping these days, so – particularly if you're travelling outside Europe – there may be air ticket discounts to be had.

Small agency or large? I used to use two old ladies, straight out of *Arsenic and Old Lace*, who were red-hot at tracking down out-of-the-way European jaunts at a few days' notice, but were somewhat out of their depth when asked to trawl south of the Bay of Naples. But the big outfit I used intermittently for more ambitious expeditions would get decidedly sniffy when asked to fix me up with anything so commonplace as a couple of tickets to the Isle of Wight. (Willingness, or lack of it, to perform small, not very profitable services is a good test of a travel

agency's worth.) In the course of time I compromised
between large and little by throwing in my lot with a
small local branch of one of the biggest agency
chains, so that I can get personal, hometown service
which is nevertheless plugged in to a vast worldwide
network of resources. I always deal with the same
assistant, a charming, bubbly girl who loves her job
and takes a real delight in tackling the impossible.
If she moves on and her place is taken by some take-
it-or-leave-it drone for whom a potentially disappointed customer isn't a challenge, then I shall
move on too. In fact if my treasure remains in the
business instead of marrying a millionaire whose
problem of getting to Singapore via Stuttgart, Oslo
and Portland, Maine, she solved with a wave of her
magic wand, I shall probably follow her anyway.
Good travel clerks are worth hanging on to.

Failing the discovery of your own travel treasure, I
would certainly give short shrift to any agency where
any of the following overheards seem likely to be
overheard:

'No, I'm sorry, it's completely booked up,
apparently.'
'Do you think you could come back tomorrow?
Only we're closing soon.'
'I'll see what we can do, but I'm afraid we can't
make any promises.'
'I'm afraid you'll have to make your own
arrangements for the rail part of the journey
when you get to Bombay.'
'I'll double-check if you like, but I don't hold any
hopes.'
'We don't do that service any more.'
'We can only make a request for the hotel of your
choice, but you must pay here and now.'
'It'd show up on the computer if there was any
space on that flight – I don't see what else I can
do.'
'I'm afraid that's against company policy.'
'I'll specify your requirements, but I can't
guarantee you'll get that particular room.'

'I'm sorry, we've been so busy I haven't been
able to get through.'
'I don't have to look it up – I know.'

Getting Organised

In the beginning is The List. You write down everything that has to be done, from buying a new bathing
suit to boarding the cat, then tick off each task as it is
accomplished. You also, in the course of working
your way through The List, add all those sup-
plementary items you had forgotten (Find suitcase
keys . . . copy out addresses for postcards . . . programme video . . . programme neighbours) until it
begins to seem that you will never get to the end of it.
These notes are intended not to make that prospect
even more remote, but to make The List a shade more
comprehensive than it perhaps sometimes is.

Passports. Before even picking up a holiday
brochure, find the family's passports. Better still,
always know where they are in the first place. Having located them, check their expiry dates – passports
have a nasty habit of running out. If any of them
needs renewing, allow ten weeks for Passport Office
incompetence or working to rule. If you read reports
of a passport application backlog, you're likely to get
quicker service at one of the regional offices. NB: if
you have any expired passports about the house,
keep them well away from those in current use,
otherwise you may find yourself in the position of a
young friend of mine on his way to San Francisco,
who presented himself at Heathrow with an out-of-
date passport half an hour before check-in time. It
took a 10p phone call and a £20 cab-ride to get him out
of trouble.

Visas. These too can take weeks. The easiest way
to get a visa is to unload the job on someone else.
Your travel agent should be able to arrange it: otherwise find another travel agent or go to a visa agency.
Expect to pay a fee of around £5 to £10 per passport
according to speed of delivery: worth it, though,

since some visa sections can be unbelievably bloody-minded. So can immigration officials at the port of entry, so make sure your visa hasn't run out, and never assume you don't need a visa anyway. A man I know got all the way from London to Sydney before learning that you need one to visit Australia – they wouldn't let him through the door and he had to go on to New Zealand to get his papers put in order. Conversely, some visas are a bar to entry into other countries. Arab League countries won't let you in if your passport says you've been to Israel. The way around this is to have two passports, which a surprising number of travellers don't realise is possible. Leave it to a visa agency to fix. But if you want to go to Mecca you have to acknowledge that there is only One God and Muhammad is His Messenger. The USA, on the other hand, are on the verge of scrapping visa requirements for short-stay visitors, which will be a far cry from my first visit to the United States when I had to go to the Embassy, raise my right hand and swear not to overthrow the United States Government.

Currency. Buy travellers' cheques or Eurocheques, of course, but also enough foreign currency to last you a couple of days should the banks be on strike or celebrating the president's birthday. Your own bank will try to palm you off with the biggest notes available, unless you specify that you want smaller denominations suitable for tipping and small transactions in cafés and shops. It is also useful to have some coins about you, but banks won't deal in foreign coins. I always hang on to any surplus coins I come home with, throwing them into a drawer for future use – which is how I always come to arrive in Paris with a mixed pocketful of francs, lire, pfennigs and cents. By the way, don't take sterling cheques to the USA, where they are regarded as on a par with glass beads.

Credit cards. These, like passports, have expiry dates. Don't find yourself trying to pay for that last splurge after the cash has run out with an out-of-date card. Note credit card hotline number in case of loss or theft.

Tickets and vouchers. Get your tickets in good time, picking them up yourself if necessary (some travel agencies, with touching faith in the first class post, leave it to the last possible moment before sending them out). Check your tickets carefully against the details on your itinerary – there is not only the possibility of human error (or computer error as it is known in the trade) but also, if you are on a charter package, a chance that your flight has been 'consolidated' – that is, combined with another part-filled flight scheduled for a different time. Here I would recommend you to turn to *Any Complaints?*, but if departure times are shifted by under 12 hours they don't have to pay compensation. If you have an all-in

Arrive in Paris with a mixed pocketful of francs, lire, pfennigs and cents

deal, you should have a voucher to present to the hotel on arrival. Make sure it's in your possession and that it's for the period specified. I have sore memories of arriving for seven days in Florence on a voucher which had me booked in for three.

Jabs. If you're going anywhere exotic, or travelling on to temperate climes *from* somewhere exotic, check whether you need injections. Because many countries no longer require vaccination certificates, it doesn't necessarily follow that your chances of contracting an unpleasant tropical disease have diminished to zero. It simply means that coming from a healthy environment you are less likely to bring it into the country. Ask your doctor or pick up the DHSS leaflet *Protect Your Health Abroad*. Frontier bureaucracy being what it is, some Third World countries still require smallpox certificates even though smallpox has been universally eliminated.

Insurance. You don't have to buy the insurance that comes with your package trip, though some tour operators will try to tell you that this form of inertia selling is bound up in the deal. But do be insured – particularly against having to cancel. You may find that your credit card company already insures you against loss and injury, if you pay for the trip with your card. But read the small print. It doesn't necessarily fulfil the promise of the big print.

Climate. To decide on what clothing you'll need, don't take the brochure's word for it that the temperature should be around 80°F and the rainy season isn't till February. Check the weather columns. If yesterday's around-the-world table says it was 60°F and bucketing down, that's the source to believe.

PS: Having finally got a master list together and ticked everything off, don't throw it away in relief. Put it in the passport drawer for use next time.

There are only two emotions in a plane:
boredom and terror.

ORSON WELLES

Packing

'It is a great convenience to take one's bath with one,' advised *Hints To Lady Travellers* in 1889. A hundred years on, there is still a nomadic tribal urge to pack everything including the kitchen sink for even the briefest hop across the Channel.

We pack too much, and particularly women pack too much. I go not only by my own observation, which is considerable, but by a survey conducted by a luggage manufacturer. Up to half the clothes women take on holiday are not used. They take new shoes which are too uncomfortable to wear, evening dresses too formal for hot weather, non-crushproof clothing that becomes too creased, and warm sweaters 'just in case'.

We have discussed (see *Getting Organised*) The List. The packing list should be a sub-division of it. But instead of expanding, as the master list does, the packing list should shrink – ideally to half its original length.

These are some items that will prove to be Not Wanted On Voyage:

More changes of underclothing than there are days in your holiday;

A business suit in case you go somewhere formal (unless you're on a business trip, that is – but all business travellers know how to pack);

A thick dull book that you've never had time to read;

Any more than two pairs of shoes – both of which should be worn in, and one of which you should already be wearing;

Ditto ties, belts, handbags and other accessories;

Enough dresses, skirts and tops to enable you to change four times a day. By all means retain the right to select from your wardrobe at whim – just work out your whims in advance, that's all, and leave the wardrobe at home;

The plug adapter set, and anything electrical to go with it. Take a small battery razor, and borrow a hair-drier from the hotel;

Enough film to shoot *Gone With The Wind*;
And go easy on the spares – toothpaste,
  batteries, sunglasses etc. Some people carry so
  many emergency spares that they are
  practically travelling in duplicate.

You should now have enough room in your suit-case for some of those items which you will wish you had packed but which completely slipped your mind, such as:

Basic first aid kit, including Band-Aid for when
  you nick your finger trying to get the plastic
  wrapping off the jam at breakfast;
Sewing kit for rips caused by squeezing past
  squadrons of motor bikes parked on pavement;
Soap (even the most de luxe of hotels often
  expect you to perform your ablutions with a
  tablet of soap the size of a butter pat);
A good thick book which you're looking forward
  to reading;
A corkscrew and a champagne stopper for
  picnics;
A compact radio on which you can get the World
  Service – programmes and frequencies in
  London Calling, BBC World Service, Bush
  House, Aldwych, London WC2;
Gadget for picking up answering machine
  messages, if you can't live without it;
A fold-up holdall in which to haul back your
  duty-frees, plus all the things which fitted
  perfectly well into your case on the way out but
  which seem to have swelled with the heat.

But not a huge box of Kleenex. Yes, the tissue container in your hotel bathroom is going to run out half-way through your visit, and no, it is never going to be replenished. But you can buy fresh supplies down the street. And there we have the key to successful packing. If you find yourself a pair of socks short, they do sell washing powder in foreign parts. They sell socks too, if you can't be bothered rinsing. Indeed, there is little that you may have forgotten or failed to include that cannot be acquired abroad if the need is really there, which usually it isn't. So there is no need to pack as for Noah's Ark.

Packing properly, one couple going away for a fortnight should be able to get everything into one moderately-sized suitcase, supplemented by a strong canvas carry-on bag for overspill items like hairbrushes, sponge bags and magazines. For a week or less, they should be able to get by on one case apiece small enough to qualify as hand baggage (18" × 14" × 6"), thus eliminating the fear of arriving with nothing but what they stand up in owing to their luggage having been left behind.

As for what you might care to pack your packing in, see the next section.

We pack too much . . .

Vanity Cases

All travellers are suitcase snobs. Their luggage's primary purpose may be to spare them from the inconvenience of carrying their belongings around in brown paper parcels, but its secondary purpose is to impress.

A good suitcase is a portable good address – with the advantage that you don't have to worry about the mortgage.

There are, to be sure, those who eschew pigskin in favour of stained and bulging canvas that looks as if it had once been crammed with severed limbs and left at the Paddington Station left-luggage office by a Victorian murderer. They are inverted suitcase snobs. 'See,' their luggage proclaims. 'Appearances matter not a jot to us. But don't we look well-travelled?'

Being seen to have travelled is, to the traveller, to have arrived. The *QE2* label, nonchalantly overlapping the P & O labels, is as important as the cruise itself. A Concorde trip is an exciting experience, but a Concorde luggage tag chained umbilically to a suitcase handle lasts forever.

There are, mind you, labels and labels. A Thomas Cook's label is fine, because it looks as if Thos himself slapped it on to identify your bags. Ditto, and with the same justification, the adhesive insignia of airline, shipping line or ferry. But an hotel label somehow carries the aura of having been begged from the concierge – or worse, bought in a souvenir shop.

In this connection, I must confess my own little weakness, for of course I am as much a suitcase snob as the next traveller. I do not collect either labels or airline tags – indeed, I am punctilious about ripping them off once they have served their purpose. Somehow or other, though, each torn-off tag manages to leave behind it the loop of string, thread or elastic that secured it to my luggage. Thus, over the years, my suitcase handles have accumulated such a wealth of stringy residue that they now feel like tennis-racquet handles. 'Behold,' my suitcases announce, as loudly as if they were broadcasting over the airport public address system, 'a seasoned traveller – but far too seasoned to draw attention to the fact.'

As to the actual bags and baggage to which all those tags and labels and bits of string are attached, or not attached as the case may be, each piece of luggage tells a story.

The soft leather suitcase, bristling with straps and buckles which convey a general aura of trenchcoat epaulets, wishes us to know that it is the property of a gentleman whose ivory hairbrushes and Jermyn Street shirts are among its contents. The smart fibreglass job tells us that it belongs to a junior executive with a concertina of credit cards in his wallet.

The zip-up carry-on plastic wardrobe boasts – brags of – a whizz-kid owner so busy and mobile and high-powered he won't have time to unpack at the other end.

A set of matching luggage in expensive patterned fabric, like a travelling three-piece suite, indicates a very senior executive who expects to be met by a limousine, and whose wife is accompanying him – on the company.

An oversized tote bag speaks of the glamorous, globe-trotting vocation of one who has time only to chuck in a few shirts and jeans before speeding to Heathrow on his next exciting mission.

And so on, as round and round and round the airport carousel these travellers' telltale grips and holdalls and cases and coffers and valises and trunks and portmanteaux trundle, and each of us, while keeping a sharp eye open for our own suitcases and praying that they will not have shamed us by bursting open, appraises the social status of each piece of luggage as it rumbles by. Tinker, tailor, soldier, traveller . . .

But who is it, apart from each other, we suitcase snobs are trying to impress? Certainly not our friends, unless we can find some excuse for conducting them into the cupboard under the stairs when they call.

The suitcase snob's first target is undoubtedly the staff of the hotel whither his suitcase accompanies him – or he accompanies it. As surely as if he were to hand over character references from his bank and the Lord Lieutenant of his county, his suitcase informs the commissionaire that he is a person of rank and substance, not some cheapskate who will slink off without tipping when he leaves. It conveys to the porter who conducts him to his room that he is perfectly at ease in this grand hotel and, as a matter of fact, is accustomed to establishments even grander. It reassures the chambermaid that he is not about to steal the towels.

Beyond the hotel portals, the suitcase has several specific functions. It warns the taxi driver that he is not dealing with a country bumpkin who can be induced to pay treble the going rate. It tips the wink to airport staff that its custodian knows his way about and so they do not have to treat him like a nervous old lady on her first flight. To the Customs man it stands surety for his honesty. To the weekend host it vouchsafes that he knows how to hold a fork. And to all and sundry it proclaims that this is no ordinary mortal who walks among them.

All in all, no traveller should leave home without it.

At the Airport

The general assumption is that airport novels are meant to be started on the aeroplane and finished on the beach. They are not. They are intended to be ploughed through at the airport itself, to fill in the endless waiting. That's why they're called airport novels.

If there is such a place as Hell, it is undoubtedly an airport with the code-tag HAD, for Hades. It is not that all airports are necessarily obnoxious, over-crowded plastic stockyards – some of the more modern or modernised ones, such as Zürich, Singapore, the newer part of Los Angeles International, and even Gatwick on a quiet day, are actually quite pleasing (Heathrow, though, I preferred when it was a collection of wooden huts). But it is the endless, aimless, exhausting, dehydrating waiting that makes

even the most sanguine of seasoned travellers wish
they had stayed at home.

To begin with, the check-in times are set far too
early – often by as much as two hours before boarding. That's the airport authority's doing: having time
to kill lures you into the International Shoppes from
which they milk their profit. (Personally, I would
never set foot in a duty-free shop. Some of the stuff is
even dearer than in the High Street, and while booze
and tobacco are undoubtedly cheaper, the only
brands available tend to be the higher-priced ones
with the designer labels and the fancy packaging.)

Then, as often as not, there is a delay in boarding.
Of any pair of flights outward and inward, I am
grateful if only one of them sets off on time. Indeed,
flight delay is so much a fact of travelling life that
when you come back from India your friends ask not
'How was the Taj Mahal?' but 'How was the flight?'

And then when there is a delay, there is no one to
give you any information beyond what may or may
not be briefly indicated on the destination board
('Wait in lounge'). Airports are staffed by utterly
passive people who never go and find out what is
wrong. When they do know what's wrong they hug
it to themselves. So the poor benighted passengers
frequently aren't made aware that there is to be a
three-hour delay until there has been a three-hour
delay.

I was once waiting to board a charter flight back to
London from Pisa. Boarding time came and went and
nothing happened – no announcement, no one at the
departure gate, no one to ask what was going on.
Pisa is a tiny airport and after an hour or so the
atmosphere was claustrophobic. We simply had no
way of finding out how long we were going to be kept
there, drinking endless thimbles of espresso, pacing
up and down and staring out of the windows for
signs of activity out on the runway. Finally I insisted
on barging my way back through passport control
and ran down our cabin crew who were hanging
about outside having a chat and a smoke. They knew
what the trouble was and readily told me – a cargo
hatch door that wouldn't shut or something of the

kind. We'd be boarding in about another half-hour.

So why couldn't they pass the glad tidings on to their passengers?

> 'We're not allowed to use the Tannoy system.'
> 'Then why don't you come through to the departure lounge and tell us?'
> 'We don't have a loudspeaker.'
> 'You don't need a loudspeaker. The departure lounge is not much bigger than my living room at home. Standing in the middle of it, and speaking in an ordinary conversational tone, you could make yourself heard to every passenger on the flight.'
> 'Yes, well there'll be an announcement when we're ready to board.'

I suppose they were only obeying the corporate instinct of airline folk that in so impersonal a centre as an airport you don't do anything so personal as addressing your flock direct except through a microphone.

The last link, and the missing one, in the chain of airport communication is communication itself. Airlines are simply hopeless at keeping their customers informed, their general demeanour being one of utter bemusement at this totally unexpected, isolated freak setback. As a matter of fact, the airlines frequently know well enough, and well in advance, which of their flights are most likely to be delayed – they have timetables projecting the potential delay on peak flights and at congested airports. In America, there has been a move to introduce legislation forcing the airlines to provide more accurate flight schedules, with fines if they are wilfully optimistic about arrival times. But even in the unlikely event of our ever having such a law on the English side of the Atlantic, it would not have saved me from the ninety-minute hold-up I once suffered while trying to get to the American side. It proved that they had omitted to load the desserts for dinner and we were waiting for supplies to arrive from the caterers. When this news leaked, there was a near-mutiny among passengers (I believe I was instrumental in fermenting it) who demanded that we jettison the puds and get moving. To no avail. The chocolate gunge with cream topping had been programmed into the system, and chocolate gunge with cream topping we were going to have.

The sheer murder of hanging around airports, aggravated by chaotic check-in queues and the presence of herds of backpackers using the departure lounge as a dormitory (why can't they put arms on the seats so that it's impossible for any one passenger to hog the space of four?), is a significant factor in the stress engendered by travel, which by the way is supposed to be on a scale somewhere between getting a divorce and moving house. How can the ordinary traveller (the extraordinary traveller can head for the VIP lounge) set about lessening the ordeal?

In the first place, by endeavouring to spend as little time in those God-forsaken halls as you can manage. If it's at all possible to check in elsewhere than the airport, do so. If not, while by all means allowing a margin for traffic hiccups, get there as near to check-in time as your agitated partner will allow. If you're constitutionally incapable of cutting it fine, set off as early as you wish but head not for the airport but for one of the airport hotels, and have breakfast or lunch there. They will shuttle you to the terminal when the time comes, and if your luck's in may even check you in.

Don't queue unnecessarily. Wanting to get check-in over and done with is understandable, but English travellers in particular will bovinely queue for anything – passport control, security, the cafeteria; they will even, bags in hand (why don't they put them *down*?) queue at the departure gate for an hour, for all that they already have their boarding passes and seat numbers. The coolest travellers find somewhere to park themselves and get on the plane last.

Travel as unencumbered as you can. Slogging around an airport – and remember the boarding gate can be nigh on half a mile from the departure lounge, and at least one of the people-movers isn't going to be working – is wearying enough in itself without a camera-case strap cutting into your shoulders, the handles of a clanking duty-free bag cutting into your fingers, your carry-on bag bumping against your hip and a stack of magazines slithering from under your arm. I sweat just to think of it.

Assuming you're travelling in company, establish a base – near the bar is as good a spot as any – where you can dump your gear. Then you can saunter off by rota to browse at the bookstall, get ripped off in the duty-free shop, check the destination indicator again, or just mooch. It passes the time.

Have something to do. If you're a crossword addict you'll never get a better opportunity. Knit. Play Travel Scrabble.

Eat if you must. That passes the time too, but allow for the food being so disgusting and the service so shambolic or indifferent (it isn't always) that the experience can only add to the suffering. Egon Ronay wages a nonstop war against the shredded paper salads, compost-heap fish pie and sawdust cakes with shaving cream topping they serve up at airports – airline food, in short, without the excuse. To which the airport catering services respond, 'Passengers don't want high cuisine – this is a shove-them-through and seat-them-fast operation.' Why so? Of all assembly points on earth, airports, behind their frenetic façade, are the most leisurely. Their customers have time hanging heavily on their hands and don't need to gulp down fast food.

Avoid aggro and agitation. As one who tends to fume and fulminate at airports, that's the advice I give myself before every journey I make, and I am afraid I do not always follow it. When I do, I try to fall into a waking coma, a resigned, listless, uncomplaining, undemanding, unexpectant state of mind such as you would find in a mollusc or at the tail-end of a mile-long queue for radio valves in Vladivostok, from which I emerge only when I am sitting in a hot bath at the other end. A friend and I once dreamed up a travel agency which for a suitable fee and at a suitable moment before our client was due to set off would approach the back of his head with a sockful of sand. He would be stacked aboard as cargo, collected by a courier at the other end, and delivered through customs and immigration to his hotel room where he would wake up to find a cocktail at his elbow.

Another way of not knowing what hit you is to start reading that airport novel.

Fear of Flying

Fear of flying is nature's way of telling you that if you are in an air crash you are likely to get killed. Statistically you have a better chance of being kicked to death by a donkey. Ten thousand scheduled airline passengers would have to fly for 10,000 miles a year each for 1,500 years before one of them was due to die in a crash. But that still leaves those who persist in flying far more vulnerable to an air crash than those who stay on the ground. That is why people who are afraid of flying are afraid of flying.

While we are bandying statistics, the airlines reckon that half of us are mildly aerophobic, with twenty per cent actively worried about flying. It is a wretched condition if it is allowed to take hold. I was once on a British Airways flight from Rome when it was visited by last-minute gremlins while we were out on the runway waiting for take-off – only a minor hitch but one needing an engineer to come out and fix it. We waited half an hour, then the man sitting next to me began to crack. I could see exactly what was in his mind because it was in mine as well: if this plane crashed, he would wish in his last seconds that he'd got off when he had the chance. He began to shake. It needed a lot of courage to display his cowardice in front of all these people, but he was adamant in demanding that they let him out. Eventually, after a great deal of palaver, a companionway was wheeled up, a cabin door was opened up and he was allowed to slink off.

Another half hour passed, then it proved that our problem was trickier than the captain had supposed. We would have to taxi back to the departure gate, and it now looked as if it would be the best part of two hours before we were ready for take-off. Now I happened to know that an Alitalia London flight was due out any minute. I had only hand baggage with me, so I sprinted for the Alitalia desk and got my transfer. And my fellow-passenger, as I settled into my seat, proved to be the same wretched fellow whose nerve had gone on that abortive BA take-off earlier. His eyes pleaded with me not to recognise him. Clearly, had he been able to choose between sitting next to me and plunging into a mountain-top on the other flight, he would willingly have gone to his doom. Maybe the experience cured him of his fear of flying.

There are several ways of dealing with aerophobia, the most obvious one being never to let your feet leave the ground. I have several friends who refuse point-blank to fly anywhere, ever – one lost a lucrative contract in Hollywood because they couldn't wait for him to arrive by boat and train.

There are therapy courses and there is hypnosis – the success rate with either seems to hinge on whether there is an underlying psychological trigger that sets off the fear, rather than straightforward panic at being five miles up in the air without a parachute. There are books – *Taking the Fear Out of Flying* (David & Charles) is by Maurice Yaffé who runs seminars on air travel anxiety and claims a high success rate.

There is also a certain number of practical steps one can take in the hope of pacifying one's fears – ask for a seat by an exit; try to assimilate the emergency instructions card before your eyes glaze over, and attend closely when the stewardess demonstrates the lifejacket (I have watched this ceremony hundreds of times, but I know if I ever had to put the damned thing on I should make a hash of it); you can even, in the spirit of Hans Christian Andersen who carried a rope with him in case he was trapped in a fire, rent or hire a portable smoke hood.

The most popular way of handling fear of flying is of course to get mildly smashed. A few stiff ones will help at first but the chemicals they put in spirits can help to create the very feelings of panic you're trying to combat. Smoking helps if you happen to smoke and have managed to get a seat in the smoking section if there is one, but not if you are a non-smoking aerophobic sitting close by. In any case it is becoming ever more difficult to find a flight on which smoking is allowed at all. It will be interesting to see what a total ban on smoking does for passengers' nerves.

Owning up to my own fear of flying, I would say that on a scale of one to ten I register about four. It was higher when I was younger and my affairs were less settled and my family had yet to grow up. I don't have the urge (quite a common one – much aero-phobia is simply claustrophobia) to yank open the door and jump out, but I do have recurrent air-crash dreams whenever I am about to fly or have just flown. I have a superstitious fear of nuns or teddy bears being aboard, arising from a composite im-pression, culled from a score of air disaster reports, of nuns comforting the survivors and a pathetic teddy bear being found among the wreckage.

I have a kind of running mantra to get me through take-off and landing – I feel relatively safe during the bit in between. I tell myself that had I been marked off by Fate as an air-crash victim it would have hap-pened years ago; that although I can bring to mind twelve people I've known who have died in car crashes and two who have died on motor bikes, plus scores who have been visited by the Grim Reaper in a variety of guises, I don't know a single soul who has died in an air crash; that the flight seems much smoother than many I could call to mind; that if there was anything wrong the stewards and stewardesses wouldn't be joshing and laughing (maybe they're hysterical?); and that the beautiful young woman across the aisle was surely not put on this earth only to be removed from it at 30,000 feet up. It helps too, I find, to be flying with someone who is even more scared than I am.

Otherwise I carry two pieces of advice about with me in case of emergency: one from a specialist in hijack psychology – 'Avoid eye contact, do as you're told and don't speak unless you're spoken to'; the other from a survivor of the Manchester United Munich disaster some years ago: 'Sit near the back and pray.'

Jet Lag

It is a pity transatlantic flight wasn't invented a couple of centuries earlier, then we'd have a host of folk remedies for jet lag.

Some of the wrinkles we do have are pretty bizarre. I know travellers who swear by wearing paper bags on their feet; they say it gets them through the time warp daisy-fresh. There may be the makings of a folk remedy in this one – after all, Howard Hughes, the eccentric founder of TWA, was noted for shuffling around with Kleenex boxes on his feet.

While there are those who claim not to suffer from it at all, there is really no way out of jet lag to some degree or another. The body clock ticking relentlessly away on home-base time in sulky resentment at your arbitrarily altering its meal, sleep and bowel-movement schedule without consultation – that plus dehydration plus travel fatigue plus airport stress (a smooth journey noticeably generates less jet lag than a hairy one): these ingredients shaken up produce a cocktail of quite distressing symptoms – lightheadedness, disorientation running to mild hallucinations and noises in the head, loss of memory, lack of appetite, indigestion, constipation, exhaustion dogged by insomnia, and a vague depression arising out of the nagging conviction that this whole trip may have been a mistake.

But if you cannot escape jet lag you can make it keep its distance. The standard, if boring, antidote is to wear loose clothes, remove shoes (take a shoehorn – feet swell in flight), cat-nap during the flight, eat sparingly, and don't touch alcohol at all but drink lots of water or fruit juice. Without doubt this regime will get you to journey's end in better shape than if you have drunk the aircraft dry. The trouble is that the sensations induced by hurtling along in a capsule six miles up in the air – euphoria, fear, boredom, excitement, gloom – are not really an incentive for going temporarily on the wagon. Pragmatically, the best available advice in this area is to take it easy – bad jet lag is part hangover.

Somewhere in the scientific pipeline there is a pill containing melatonin, a hormone at present only non-commercially produced in the brain and released into the body during sleep. The biochemistry team working on it say that when we travel across time zones, the melatonin in our bodies can take up to a week to adjust. A melatonin pill would push the body clock backwards or forwards as required. Make sure, when it comes on the market, you don't take the wrong one.

Meanwhile, other scientists experimenting with hamsters, which until now I did not know had a jet lag problem, recommend a bout of strenuous activity after a flight – jogging, for instance. ICI tells its executives to go for a two-mile walk on arrival. Presumably they can take their bleepers.

Yet others swear by diet. A self-addressed envelope (no need for a stamp) to Anti-Jet Lag Diet, Argonne National Laboratory, 9700 South Cass Avenue, Argonne, Illinois 60439, will get you their pre-take-off diet, too complicated to reproduce here but basically a three-day regime of alternating feast days and fast days programmed to whether you're travelling east or west. Argonne is one of the US Department of Energy's major research centres and I am impressed no end by their work on the daily biological rhythms of animals. A badger flying backwards and forwards across the Atlantic would do well to heed their advice.

For myself, I do not have a jet lag cure but I do have a jet lag palliative. My routine during the flight is to eat moderately, which I do not find difficult since most airline food is despicable; drink as moderately as maybe; take plenty of water (this not only keeps the alcohol intake down but helps cope with the aircraft's low humidity); walk up and down the plane a lot (helps circulation); and sleep through the movie.

Once at the hotel, I shower and change, have a swim if there's a pool available, a short stroll if there isn't, and thereafter fall in as much as possible with the local rhythm, drinking at my usual pace but confining the food intake to a light, brasserie-type meal. No work beyond a few telephone calls. I usually finish the evening in a jazz club, staying awake until the body clock, not to mention my own watch which I have kept on GMT, reminds me that it is getting on for six in the morning our time. I'm by then so pleasantly fatigued I can sleep a full eight hours without a break. I awake feeling thoroughly refreshed, though for the first couple of days I do make a point of having a cat-nap before going out for the evening.

The return journey, without the boost of excitement always generated by travel to foreign parts however familiar they have become, is more of a problem. My solution, such as it is, is to fall onto an evening flight after a roisterous lunch and immediately go to sleep, or anyway try to. I usually succeed in dozing intermittently through the night, but even if kept awake by the babe in arms behind me who seemingly follows me about the world, I have nothing else to eat or drink except water until breakfast time. The day of arrival I write off completely, devoting it to slumping about the house, catching up with the newspapers and watching television. Around four o'clock I have a two-hour nap and wake up to a shower and a stiff vodka martini, after which I feel as right as ninepence, or anyway eightpence halfpenny.

But I would never claim not to suffer from jet lag. I have only ever met one man I've completely believed when he assured me that in a lifetime of crossing the Atlantic he's never suffered from a moment's jet lag. This walking wonder put it down to a sensible regime and the fact that he was the captain of the *QE2*.

BEING
THERE

Useful Phrases
(*for the travelling companion*)

'We're on *holiday*, for God's sake!'
'I thought you said you could get by in Spanish.'
'I don't know what was wrong with the first bar we saw.'

'So much for your famous sense of direction.'

'How was I supposed to know it's closed on Sundays?'

'I did tell you the coach was leaving at nine sharp.'

'But I thought *you* wrote down the address.'

'Of course we don't have to book.'

'You know you don't like squid, so why did you order it?'

'Can't you ever manage to get us chairs by the pool?'

'You're not seriously suggesting I climb up all those steps?'

'Why is it impossible to get a decent cup of tea?'

'Serves you right for staying up half the night swigging margaritas – you know you can't drink.'

'Must you keep eyeing the waiter?'

'You do realise we're being charged five hundred per cent more for a teaspoonful of coffee than at that perfectly nice place last night?'

'If you can't bring yourself to utter one word of the bloody language, could you at least stop saying "Thanks awfully, you're so kind" when they fetch you the English mustard?'

'If you ask me anything, one Roman amphitheatre looks much like another.'

'For heaven's sake, it's a plaster replica – they must turn these things out by the thousand.'

'Let's face it, what we're staying in is an industrial suburb.'

'Have you ever given any thought to separate holidays?'

At the Hotel

A few years ago, returning late at night to my hotel in Bristol, I asked the dinner-jacketed fellow behind the desk, whom I took to be the night receptionist, to give me a call at seven with early-morning tea.

The request did not go down well. 'I happen,' he said frostily, 'to be the banqueting manager.'

'In that case,' I said, 'I would like a call at seven with early morning tea for 350 people.'

The misunderstanding would not arise now, for when I stayed at that same hotel again recently, there were tea-making 'facilities' in the room, and you punched out a number on the telephone to get your alarm call – a recorded voice like the speaking clock.

If these are improvements, and I suppose they are when you consider that the tea used to arrive cold and half an hour late, then hotels (and particularly British ones) may certainly be said to have improved over the years, and clearly they wish to improve even more, since in many hotel rooms these days you find a 'guest questionnaire' requesting 'one moment of your time' to tick off boxes indicating whether your reception was wonderful, less than wonderful, or only fairly wonderful, and so on. I don't know whether anyone ever answers these questionnaires – I know I don't, since the only two questions I would bother with are never listed. These are: *a*, what did you find broken? and *b*, what did you find missing?

It is rarely that I have set my suitcase down without encountering an irritating minor deficiency of some sort in my room. On the breakages front, there is almost invariably a lamp that won't work. Sometimes the TV is on the blink, sometimes the lavatory flushes imperfectly, sometimes the coffee-maker won't make coffee, and if only I could figure out how to work the while-U-sleep trouser-press, that's probably broken too. As for items that should have been replaced and haven't been, tissues head the list, followed by laundry sacks, sachets of coffee for the broken coffee-maker, and a mini-bottle or two (which will go on the bill if you don't watch out) from the minibar. Efficient hotels issue a check-list of everything that could need repair or replacement, but inefficient hotel staff fail to follow it. I would gladly do the job myself if only they would stop asking me if I found my room fit for a king, fit for a prince, or only fit for a duke.

But we are off on the wrong foot here. I like hotels, with their Gideon Bibles and shoe-polishing machines and alarming fire regulations and printed cardboard pyramids offering sauna baths and candle-lit dinners and conference suites; and I like hotel rooms, even though they too often give the impression of having been designed by someone who has never stayed in one.

There is always a sense of excitement as the porter unlocks the room door (or, more often these days, as you unlock it yourself). Will the spirits sink or soar? Will it be an L-shaped cupboard overlooking the stairwell, or will it be square and spacious with a sofa and chintzy armchairs and a dressing table that isn't screwed to the wall, and an exciting view? With the right room, the right bathroom (a shower with the force of a fire hose and a stack of complimentary shampoos, oils and unguents), and the right lobby – I love those bustling American hotel lobbies with news-stands and barber shops and cigar kiosks – I could happily live in a hotel.

You can tell in an instant whether you and your room are going to hit it off. For a bad experience, first impressions don't have to be as traumatic as those of a friend staying in quite a posh hotel in Manchester, who drew back his curtains to reveal only a stretch of wall – there were no windows. An air of indefinable gloom is enough to identify an inferior room. The gloom signifies that you are at the back of the hotel, as likely as not next to the clattering lift shaft and certainly within earshot of the central plumbing. A bright room, indicating that you are at the front, will nearly always be a nice room – simply because the front is where the best rooms are.

There is no need to be fatalistic about a bad room. Flatly refuse to have anything to do with it and march back to reception. Particularly have nothing to do with it if it is not the kind of room you have specified.

In rejecting an unacceptable room, it is important not to leave your bags in it while they are sorting things out. Just as possession is nine points of the law, so a room with bags in it is regarded by hotel management as nine points occupied, and they will drag their heels over finding another room.

An element of fatalism is more in order, however, when it comes to the service. Room service is either fast or slow, and there is little you can do about it short of resolving not to use it again. Fulminate to your heart's content, by all means, but bad room service is usually a matter of flaws in management strategy which you are not going to iron out by asking just how long it takes to make a smoked salmon sandwich, for God's sake. I have stayed in hotels where preposterous delays in room service have been accounted for by the explanation that all the waiters were busy serving lunch. Told that lunch was what I myself had been awaiting for over an hour, they would shrug – you could sense them shrugging down the telephone – and explain that it was management policy to serve dining room guests first. You cannot fight management policy. In such a situation, it is between indignation and self-catering.

So far as service of the room, as distinct from room service, is concerned, a sure way of finding your bed still unmade upon returning from lunch is to leave one of those PLEASE MAKE UP ROOM signs hanging on your doorknob. I have never known an instance where this sign wasn't completely ignored. Abroad, the maids probably think it reads DO NOT DISTURB. At home, they regard it as impertinence. If I really want my room made up early I call the housekeeper and tell her I am about to have an important business meeting in my room. This sometimes works.

Service generally – meals, drinks, late-night sandwiches – is very much in the lap of the gods. Utter incompetence has to be endured if the staff simply aren't properly trained, but I don't see why it has to be a subject for that hearty joshing so typical of hotel staff who don't know their jobs. In a hotel I stayed at in Harrogate, acquiring a bottle of champagne involved the porter in nine separate expeditions for glasses, tray, ice bucket and so on, his only comment after twenty minutes of shambling backwards and forwards being that he would forget his head if it were loose.

Hotels are at their best at breakfast time. A hotel breakfast is a very good way of starting the day – ideal when eaten on your own balcony, or on a vine-covered terrace overlooking gardens or water. It's intriguing to see what other nations have for break-fast, and I always (there's usually no option anyway, unless you don't mind cornflakes figuring on your bill as an extra) fall in with the local breakfast cuisine of bread rolls or cheese or sausage or ham or scram-bled eggs with an English muffin. The English muffin, of course, indicates that we are in America, where there is probably an enormous queue for breakfast because there's a convention in town. I don't think I've ever set foot in an American hotel of any size without finding the lobby milling with men and women in loud blazers sporting plastic name tags on their lapels. In Boston, it was a convention of barbershop quartets, who occupied every possible nook and cranny to rehearse 'Swanee' and 'There's an Old Mill by the Stream'. In Oklahoma City, it was a convention of blind people whose name tags were in Braille. In Los Angeles, it was a convention for conventioneers – the convention trade having its own convention. No matter: there's always a coffee shop down the street, and at least the coffee will be prompt. Hotel breakfasts nowadays tend to be buffet affairs, with only the coffee being served at your table. It is easier to pass through the eye of a needle than to catch the waitress's eye when you want a second cup of coffee with your buffet breakfast.

But there I go complaining again. I have stayed in many splendid hotels, and by no means all of them Hotel Splendides, though I have nothing against five-star treatment. If possible, on the principle of better the devil you know, I stay at hotels I'm already familiar with – not an infallible guarantee of a good billet, however, since it is a tendency of hotels to be owned by a different group every time you go there, and it does sometimes turn out that what you remember as a discreet, shabbily-elegant, dear old-fashioned place has been refurbished for the worse.

I like the kind of hotels that try to keep up a homely or at any rate a clubby atmosphere, and I like to feel at home in my room. Some travellers live out of their suitcases – even if they're here for a week, their rooms give the impression that they're leaving tomorrow. I like the hotel room to look lived in, with the suitcases tucked away out of sight and hair-brushes on the dressing table and magazines on the coffee table and spare ties hung up in the wardrobe instead of slung across the back of a chair. I know a woman who even brings in her own flowers if there are none provided by the management. She says it makes the room look more like her own bedroom. I wonder if, when she gets back home, she puts an after-dinner mint on her pillow?

The great and recurrent question about abroad is, is it worth getting there?

ROSE MACAULAY

Any Complaints?

You do not want to spend your entire holiday writing furious letters in your head to the airline/tour operator/hotel headquarters about the imbeciles they employ. Nor do you want to put up with whatever the imbeciles may have wished upon you. So the best time to get your complaints dealt with is as they arise. Any letters in your head should be about subsequent compensation.

Starting with the airline, the worst thing that can happen to you is that they won't let you on the plane. This means that they have overbooked and are proposing to bump you off the flight. Have nothing to do with this proposal, even when offered a bribe to take another flight (unless you could do with the money – Californian students make a handsome living picking up the hundred-dollar compensation for being bumped off weekend flights to Honolulu which they had not the slightest intention of taking anyway). If you make enough fuss, refusing to budge from the ticket counter to make way for other passengers, calling for supervisors and inventing reasons why it is absolutely imperative that you should catch this flight, then instead of being bumped off you will with any luck be bumped up to a superior class.

If you're a packaged rather than a private traveller, bumping off is less likely to be a problem, unless what you have in mind is bumping off the tour operator who has led you to an unfinished or inferior hotel. Refuse to set foot in it, except to despatch a fax to the Association of British Travel Agents (01-637 0713) of which it is to be hoped the agency which arranged your trip is a member. It will turn out that the fax operator is off with a bad back, but the mere threat, if your luck holds, will see you transferred to a better class of premises. If your courier is as stubborn as you are (and some of them can be pretty stroppy, particularly towards the end of the season) or suffering from bureaucratic inertia, go to the local tourist authority, which has a vested interest in satisfied customers, and more to the point, carries clout. But remember that you get what you pay for. Whatever the brochure says about your budget hotel (see *How to Speak Brochurese*) it is not going to be the Negresco – unless, of course, it is such a dump and you make such a fuss that you get yourself bumped up to the Negresco.

Assuming that your hotel is one whose threshold you are prepared to cross, there may still be pitfalls. Beware the hotel where the receptionist refers you to a managerial person who gushes forward with an effusive welcome. You may depend upon it that he is about to say, 'We have a problem.'

Stare him out. You do not have a problem. *He* has a problem. What he means is that he has overbooked and he is going to try putting you in the annexe. Refuse to go. It is an axiom of foreign travel that the nicer and more comfortable the hotel, the nastier and bleaker will be the annexe connected to it by a windowless corridor (although once in Sorrento, after refusing point-blank to be led like a pit pony into the annexe, and more or less hijacking the room of an unfortunate couple who had yet to turn up, I found that I had passed up a delightful little villa set in its own courtyard within the hotel grounds, and over-looking the Bay of Naples. The unfortunate couple were suitably grateful). If you have a courier, call her. Otherwise stand your ground. Pay no attention to the manager's protestations (you will by now, if you made the requisite amount of fuss, be dealing with the real manager rather than the minion earlier pass-ing himself off as the manager). Every hotel keeps back at least one good room for emergencies – and a troublemaker refusing to be budged out of the lobby is an emergency. If he will not give way, ask for the use of the hotel fax machine and frame a strong protest to the hotel chain's public relations adviser. The missive will not go off but neither will you be dumped in the annexe, and when you come back from dinner you may even find a bowl of cellophane-wrapped fruit in your room.

We have now got you to the destination of your choice and hopefully into a room you approve of. If you do not approve of it, see *At the Hotel* for further instructions. Now what else have you to complain about? A good deal, probably, but we must keep in mind the pokerwork motto that used to adorn the parlour walls of seaside boarding houses: 'God give me the power to change those things that ought to be changed, the patience to withstand those that cannot be changed, and the wisdom to know the difference.' There is no point, now you've arrived, in complain-ing about the weather, the environment, the crowds, the fact that whatever you've come to see most is closed for restoration, the noise in the street below or the smell of drains – except to your travelling com-panion, and even then in moderation. Complain about the food by all means, if you have a case, but do not complain in Greece about the food being cold – all Greek food is cold – or in Leningrad about the service being slow – all Soviet restaurant service is slow – or in Egypt about the food being terrible – all Egyptian food is terrible.

If you have a really concrete grievance such as

being short-changed or over-charged and you can't get satisfaction on the spot, go to the tourist authority (address from one of those tourist kiosks with a lower-case *i* over it) rather than the police, who will keep you all day. Going back to any dissatisfaction you may have with the holiday you've paid for, it will be a pity if you can't get it settled while you still have a holiday to enjoy, but if you can't, and you look for compensation on your return, and the tour operator begs leave to argue the toss as tour operators tend to do, write to the Conciliation Officer, ABTA, 55–57 Newman Street, London W1P 4AH. Or go to the Small Claims Court. But do have a good case. One indignant traveller demanded that the ABTA should get him compensation for being unable to use his expensive camera on safari because the zebra moved too quickly.

The British Consulate (see *Here Be Dragons*) will not want to know you unless you look like becoming an embarrassment to your host country – certainly, in the event that your hotel is but a building site or your rented apartment lacks windows, the Consulate is unlikely to run to a Double-glazing Secretariat or Wall-plastering Mission.

The English tourist is always happy abroad as long as the natives are waiters.

ROBERT MORLEY

Here Be Dragons

While not many of the disasters projected in *25 Excuses for Staying Put* are likely to befall you, going abroad must be regarded as a little more hazardous than crossing the road.

Crossing the road, indeed, is the first hazard you are likely to encounter. It is prudent to go on the assumption that the motorist hurtling towards you has murderous intentions. You must keep it in mind that any arrangement of black and white stripes and green man signs by which you may attempt to cross a busy road does not have the validity of a zebra crossing and affords no sanctuary. Getting from one side of the street to the other requires a battle of wills between the pedestrian and the oncoming traffic. My own way of emerging the victor, which I hesitate to recommend, is to avoid eye contact with the demented motorists hurtling towards me and walk firmly across to the screech of brakes. A less rash method is to join a surge of pedestrians who look like natives and must therefore be presumed to know what they are doing. By way of reassurance, in most countries it is quite a serious offence to knock you down, though in others less so.

The chances of being mugged, provided you do not walk up dark alleys by night and avoid areas notorious for that kind of thing (why don't modern street maps, like the 'here be dragons' maps of old, mark out the danger areas with warning symbols?) may be slight – but you must never assume it can't happen to you. I was once mugged in broad daylight, on a busy Saturday afternoon, outside a department store in the main shopping street of downtown Dallas.

If your guide book contains a woolly sentence to the effect that 'all cities have a crime problem, and this one is no exception' you are being warned that the place is seething with handbag thieves and pickpockets. Tour couriers, en route from the airport to the hotel, often hand out typewritten notes which are somewhat at odds with the purple prose of the official tour literature. While the party line rhapsodises over the friendly people and the relaxing atmosphere, the local cadre advises curtly, 'Push away gypsy children. Do not carry your passport, valuables and travel documents unless strictly necessary. Carry money sufficient only for the day. Keep a tight hold on your handbag. Be wary in crowds.'

This is sound advice. Should you, as a result of not taking it, find yourself without funds, return tickets, passport or all three, then you will have to go to the British Consulate, where you will be treated as a cretin at best and a sponger at worst. Consuls, who repatriate all of 350 Brits a year out of a travelling total of 27 million, do not like dealing with stranded travellers but it is one of the jobs they are there for, so do not put up with any nonsense. If it is only money you have lost, try to arrange for your credit cards to be excluded from the haul. It is at a time like this that you'll be glad you didn't leave home without them, nor kept them in the same pocket as your cash. NB: insurance companies, too, are beginning to take a distinctly consular view over paying up where the mulcted traveller has acted irresponsibly – for instance the Mediterranean swimmer who left £800-worth of francs in his clothes and returned to shore to find it gone.

Another kind of robbery is the rip-off variety. Street prices, or rather gutter prices, of the local leather goods or soapstone effigies of the Virgin Mary are not necessarily below shop or market stall prices. Compare before you buy. Street traders, like the cafés, bump up their prices according to the location of their pitch. Thus if you insist on buying a light-up gondola, it will cost you more under the arches of the Doge's Palace than in a little shop on some back canal.

On many beaches abroad, the expression 'Help! Help!' is not understood. Before entering treacherous waters, it is advisable to check with the lifeguard, if you are able to distract his attention from the two girls from Birmingham whose cigarettes he is lighting, and come to some arrangement about the signal to be employed should you be attacked by creatures

You will be treated as a cretin . . .

of the deep or caught in dangerous foreign currents. If you yourself hear the expression 'Help! Help!' while bathing, it will be the two girls from Birmingham being chased by the lifeguard.

Should the street or square on which you are staying be named after a date on the calendar, and you hear the sound of breaking glass accompanied by cries which you translate as 'Only a government of workers and intellectuals can unite our peoples and further the cause of peace and solidarity,' followed by coughing, retching, the stench of tear-gas, the whinnying of riot police horses, and occasional gunfire, it is possible that you are caught up in a revolution. Do not attempt to photograph it – the Press pay far less than you might imagine for Instamatic snaps of far-off countries of which we know little. Do not get out on your balcony, where, if sufficient students with beards are gathered under it, there is a danger that you may be compromised into making a speech, which could result in your being elected President by popular acclaim.

Statistically, the hazard you are likeliest to come up against on foreign shores is an upset tum. This is one of those rare occasions where cure is better than prevention, for no matter how many routine precautions you take – never eating unwashed or unpeeled fruit, sticking to mineral water and not buying savoury snacks at unsavoury street stalls – a stray bug can still get you. What you want is a strong preparation that does the trick immediately. Never travel without a tried and tested cure – there are several patent ones available. If you do find yourself without your bottle of Cloggo, a chemist will mix you something – but locating the late-night chemist can be a time-consuming business, especially if you have to keep dashing back to the hotel. Furthermore, doctors say that chemists' preparations can in themselves be a source of tum trouble. But they would, wouldn't they?

Finally, and harking back to crime, it may befall you by the Trevi Fountain or in the Luxembourg Gardens or in the Vienna Woods that you are approached by a ruefully apologetic fellow-countryman, well-dressed, well-spoken, who will explain how all his money has been stolen. He has telephoned home for more – there is no problem – but while waiting for the draft to arrive he is penniless, and in sore need of a meal. Could you possibly . . .? Deal with him as you wish, according to how benignly you are looking upon the world that day; but my reply is always, 'Sorry – I gave at the Eiffel Tower.'

The Plumbing

Foreign loos have lost many of their terrors – except, surprisingly enough, in the hygiene-conscious United States where the standard of rest facilities, as they like to call them, in hotels and restaurants has markedly deteriorated over the years – probably because of the number of incontinent conventioneers now swarming about.

Nowadays it is not so much the loos that are strange – those porcelained holes in the ground with foot-treads on either side – as the fancy hand-driers and bafflingly automated hand-washing gimmicks – 'To have water put hands under tap' – which have the air of having been sold to the manager by his brother-in-law.

Generally speaking the loos in hotels and good-class restaurants across the world are acceptable these days, certainly better than you'd find in the average English pub. Obviously, the more off the beaten track you stray, the more primitive will be the arrangements. If the need arises I always use any hotel that happens to be in the vicinity. They don't seem to mind being used as public lavatories. But to be on the safe side it's always as well to carry Kleenex and the odd sachet of soap-impregnated freshen-up tissues.

The hotter the clime, the more likely it is that your bathwater supply will be cut off from time to time, typically without warning. Look out for obscurely-placed notices in the lobby announcing that 'with regret the manager must cease the water from 1400 hr to 1900, this due to small of supply in tank'.

Despite what I say below about the price of a Perrier, it is not always a good idea to drink the tap water. What may be safe for the natives might not be safe for someone with no resistance to the local bacteria. Buy a bottle of the local mineral water from a shop and keep it in your room. If the room runs to a minibar, make ice with mineral water too. But there is no need to go to the lengths of a friend of mine who set his toothbrush on fire while trying to sterilise it with a bookmatch.

How they hate us, these foreigners. In Belgium as much as in France! What lies they tell of us; how gladly they would see us humiliated!

W. M. THACKERAY

Don't Drink the Champagne

'Don't drink the water' was once imperative advice to travellers. Now, 'Don't buy the water' would be more to the point – at least in the boulevard café or hotel bar, where the price of a small Perrier recalls the Weimar Republic where you trundled your loose change about in a wheelbarrow.

But then drinking almost anything abroad, from coffee to Campari, is likely to come expensive. There are still pockets such as Portugal where they practically give the wine away, but as the long shadow of tourism falls across the world, barmen of all nations are hastily revising their prices in an upward direction.

Imported spirits – gin, whisky, vodka, rum, and any but the local rough brandy – are going to be outrageously priced, no matter how the currency fares against the pound. So are imported mixers. Champagne is universally and fiendishly expensive, even in the Champagne region, unless you buy it from a wine shop to take on a picnic. The thriftiest way is to acquire a taste for the local aperitif, often an acceptable Kir-like concoction.

In restaurants, never even look at the wine list except as literature. It would be a crime, regardless of cost, not to drink the wine of the region, and that is what the reasonably-priced house wine will be – unless, of course, the district doesn't produce wine, but stick to the house wine nevertheless unless you feel like splashing out.

In cafés you pay according to the ambience, the view, the quality of the passing show and the management's inflated ideas of itself. Naturally you will want to spend an hour at Florian's, Harry's Bar or *Les Deux Magots*, but thereafter, unless you have a bottomless pocket, it would be as well to seek out a small bar or café away from the mainstream to use as your regular drinking base. It is always satisfactory to come across some little place down a back alley or in a quiet piazza which is mainly (but not entirely – you wouldn't feel comfortable) used by locals, and even more satisfactory when the bill turns out to be a tenth of what you would have paid out on the main square. The reason Italians stand up to drink their coffee, by the way, is not that they're in a hurry but that it costs a good deal more to sit down.

Hotel minibars are the most expensive means ever devised for dispensing drinks. Have nothing to do with your minibar except for storing picnic goodies and chilling the wine you have brought in from that crowded little delicatessen which appears to occupy a hole in a wall. You will, of course, have brought a corkscrew (see *Packing*).

Not Safe In Taxis

There is not a traveller alive who does not have a clutch of taxi horror stories. I will detain you with only one of mine. I picked up a cab in Greenwich Village and asked to be taken to the World Trade Center. 'Where's that?' asked the driver (I won't attempt the accent).

'It is those two 110-storey towers ahead of you.'

'How do I get there?'

'You drive towards them.'

The next thing I knew we were hurtling at great speed along Sixth Avenue in utterly the wrong direction. I rapped the bulletproof glass.

'Where the hell are you taking me?'

'Lincoln Center.'

'I don't want to go to Lincoln Center. I want to go to the World Trade Center.'

'Where's that?'

Outside England it is always wise to assume that your taxi driver is a psychopath. Many of New York's cabbies, if you can find one (their numbers have remained unchanged since 1937), are beyond doubt certifiably mad. Those who are relatively harmless cannot speak English and don't know where anything is. Elsewhere, from Rome to Rangoon, the kind of personalities you normally see shouting at themselves or directing traffic are instead all driving taxis.

The first rule about taxis is not to take one if you can possibly help it – especially from the airport (there is always a coach service into town). Many airports and railway stations carry notices warning against unauthorised drivers touting for custom. In fact, while I would not advise risking a pirate cab, I have had better rides from some pirates than I have had from many regular cab drivers, who are past masters at going the long way round. Even if you are familiar with the direct route and order them to take it, they will assure you it is clogged up with traffic as they blandly head into a five-mile tailback.

Once established at your hotel, it is worthwhile spending a little time trying to figure out the public transport system. Even the most complex bus and metro maps (after you have savoured the adventure of tracking one down) begin to make sense with a little perseverance. Using public transport is a good way of getting the feel of the place, and makes you feel almost like one of the locals. It's also rather fun mastering strange ticket machines or finding that you have to buy your bus tokens from the tobacco kiosk.

But naturally, you will not fancy travelling on an empty subway through a no-go area at two in the morning, or using the bus when the only available space is on the roof; so that brings us back to taxis. If you must take one, here are one or two things to remember.

Before hailing a cab, make sure you have plenty of change, because you may be sure the driver has not, or so he will profess.

If you do not speak the language, write your destination down in block capitals and hand it to the driver. If he doesn't know where it is, make him look it up on his map. If he doesn't have a map, get out of the cab.

If you are going a long distance – out to the catacombs or wherever – make the driver quote a price before you set off.

Make sure the meter is on. If you have to remind the driver to switch it on, it is fair to assume that you are dealing with a crook. If the meter is on but still

Write it down in block capitals and hand it to the driver

showing the previous fare, then you know you are dealing with a crook.

Don't chat up the driver – particularly don't ask him if it's very far to the zoo or the museum or some other place you plan to visit. You will find that you have made a friend of an albatross who for the rest of your journey will pester you to allow him to become your personal driver at very reasonable rates.

Don't be afraid to remonstrate if you know you are being taken on a roundabout route or the driver doesn't know where he is going – but wait until you are in a safe area. I was once unceremoniously dumped on a piece of waste ground crawling with Chicago Skid Row winos after pointing out to the driver that we had now passed the Wrigley Building three times.

Most cab drivers around the world are responsible to an authority which may deprive them of their badges in case of serious transgression. While it is a great bore lodging an official complaint against over-charging, say, it is usually enough to make a show of writing down the driver's number and the address of the cab authority. If you have a dispute and there is a policeman in sight, offer to call him over (don't actually do it unless you have to, or you may spend the rest of the day hanging around the police station while your statement is laboriously processed). But by far the most effective way of dealing with a swindling taxi driver is to put the ball in his court by paying him only what you think the journey is worth and asking what he intends to do about it. Recommended only if help is within reach or you are handy with your fists – remember that you are not dealing with a rational human being.

None of these rules, it goes without saying, applies to the renowned London cabbie who has to undergo a rigorous knowledge test of the capital's streets and main buildings before he earns the right to tell you that he is only going east.

Funny Money

I have met Americans who have been all the way round the world without ever soiling their hands on any currency other than the once almighty dollar. They hold that their dollar travellers' cheques, credit cards and actual greenbacks are negotiable currency worldwide. So they are: but if you are going to treat the world as merely another branch of Nieman Marcus, you may as well stay at home.

Part of the pleasure of being abroad is handling their funny money, of trafficking in grubby little notes worth twopence halfpenny, or grandiose ones elaborately engraved with portraits of heroes of the Second Revolution and pictures of large, multi-columned buildings, all in startling purple, and worth fivepence; of finding telephone tokens and what look like tap washers in one's change; of gradually acquiring pocketfuls of shiny coins emblazoned with strange emblems, the size and substance of medals for bravery.

But no foreign currency is so exotically strange that it cannot be mastered in a few minutes. I hate to see travellers proffering a handful of coins, like beggars in reverse, for the trader to dip into, just because they cannot be bothered to learn that there are a hundred new *glots* in a new *zprot*, and that this little zinc chap here is a 25-*glot* piece.

As for converting the prices into sterling, rather than try to read one's pocket calculator in the blinding sun, or do complicated sums in one of those little graph-paper notebooks one always seems to acquire abroad, it's easy enough to remember the basic rounded-up equivalents. For instance, the pound is worth 2,300 lire as I write, so if I round it up to 2,500 and call 500 lire twenty pence, I shan't be far out.

I'm bound to say that funny money is not quite as much fun as when we had stringent currency exchange controls. Then, with every British traveller on a limited budget, it was always a joy to watch one's fellow countrymen furtively counting their change under the table to see if they could afford a cognac with their coffee. The back-up of credit cards has taken some of the zest out of the daily ceremony of totting up one's remaining currency and dividing it by the number of days still unexpired, usually an alarming projection leading to a stern resolve to lunch off a cheese sandwich. But the ritual, swivelling the traveller between anxiety and relief as first he calculates that he is already overspending by 200 francs a day but then remembers the 500-franc note secreted in his airline ticket folder, is still one of the small pleasures of being abroad. It is always nice to find, by virtue of having had one or two cheap meals and started taking your aperitifs away from the main square, that the daily average of available currency has appreciably risen and you can resume splashing out a little.

On a bank managerial note, your calculations should always allow for having a little contingency fund left over at the end of the trip, for unexpected items like airport taxes and having another couple of beers while you scan the runway for signs of the flight you should have been on an hour ago arriving from London.

Do bear in mind that the funnier the money, the more likely it is that the territory you are visiting may impose all manner of restrictions on taking their own currency (yours too, for that matter) in and out of the country. Check with the bank. One does tend to think that because the money is funny they can't be serious, but I do know a man who thought he was doing the Italians a favour by taking in a million lire in cash to spend among them, and they not only confiscated everything above the then legal limit of 200,000 lire, but took four hours over the paperwork.

Tipping

The verb to tip is an irregular one around the world. In Japan, you don't tip taxi drivers. In Iceland, you don't tip anybody. In the USSR you're not supposed to, but you do if nobody's looking. In France, you tip theatre ushers. In the United States, some restaurants expect you to tip both the waiter and the captain or *maître d'*. In the Middle East, there are functionaries hanging around hotels and restaurants who seem to have no role other than to accept tips.

Best consult your guide book. But just as they always underestimate what you can reckon on paying for a meal, guide books always underestimate what you ought to tip; so as to how much, ask your tour courier. If in doubt, bear in mind that generally, those who expect to be tipped make their expectations known. Porters hover, coach drivers place their caps in a strategic position, cloakroom attendants have a saucer of coins of twice or even four times the denomination of the local going rate.

Hotels, particularly in eastern climes, are often milling with uniformed hangers-on opening doors, commandeering luggage and so on. I make a practice of tipping only the man who physically handles my bags. I tip the doorman for whistling up a cab, and if

You have left too much

the head porter has performed any services for me such as getting theatre tickets, I tip him at the end of the trip. The custom of leaving something for the chambermaid seems to be dying out, along with the custom of chambermaids doing more than just making the bed and changing the towels; but I do sometimes press a little something into the maid's hand should I come across her at the *beginning* of my stay, to induce her to make up my room first thing rather than in the middle of the afternoon. Hotel restaurant staff don't expect anything for meals such as breakfast that you don't have to sign for – the service is built in – but otherwise check whether the service is *compris* (in America, it never is). Hotel barmen do expect something, whether you sign the bill or pay in cash. Beyond the hotel, restaurants make it clear whether the service is included or not. Britain is the only country which adds a built-in service charge and then expects another tip on top of it. It is civil, though, to leave the small change after you have settled your bill. If the waiter bows you into the street, you have left too much – remember, when leaving what may seem a trifle when converted into your own hard currency, that in these parts it may keep a family of three for a week. As the notice in West German dining cars rather sinisterly points out, 'Prices in foreign currency are not worked out equivalently, but rather do they reflect the economic stability of the country concerned.'

As to that vexing question of just how much to tip, perhaps the tour courier isn't such a good idea after all, since she never tips anybody. For bag-carriers, taxi-whistlers and their ilk, the highly-acceptable American dollar bill might have been invented as the basic gratuity. Otherwise, keep a stock of local coins roughly equivalent to the 50p piece. Make sure you're giving the right coin – there are some shiny units of currency, often with holes in the middle, which turn out to be worth about an eighth of a penny. (On the other side of the coin, so to speak, I don't expect I have been forgotten by the Miami cabbie I tipped a hundred-dollar bill in the dark, believing it to be a dollar.)

Airport and railway porters should be tipped a dollar per piece handled – particularly kerbside check-in attendants, unless you want your baggage to travel east while you are travelling west.

As She Is Spoke

English is spoken by more people in more countries than any other language. Nearly seven times as many speak English than speak French, over fourteen times as many than speak German. That is why the French and Germans speak English while the English won't learn French or German.

We mean to, of course. As holiday time approaches we get out the learn-as-you-drive language course cassettes we bought last year and put them on the hall table, ready to take out to the car when we will become fluent in a foreign tongue at the rate of five phrases per mile. We may even think seriously about finding out where to take lessons. But once again we will depart from Heathrow linguistically equipped with no more than our smattering of schoolboy French and the menu Italian we have picked up at our local pizzeria.

So once again it is back to the old phrase book. But the trouble is that phrase books have not progressed much since the days when British consulates were besieged by travellers whose postilions had been struck by lightning.

It is not that the phrases are not bang up to date (well, perhaps not all of them. An Italian phrase book I am looking at, published 1985, has 'Give me a box of chewing tobacco,' 'I need a bottle of ink' and 'I'd like an axe' among its useful phrases). It is that the picaresque adventures which they portray are so outlandish and surrealistic that the traveller they have in mind must have a visa for Alice's Wonderland in his passport.

Taking one recent phrase book at random – a German one, but it could be any language – we first meet our wandering hero as he arrives at his hotel. At first, he is favourably impressed. His every wish, it seems, is their command. 'May I have an ashtray, bath towel, extra blanket, some envelopes, more hangers, ice cubes, extra pillow, reading-lamp, soap, writing paper?' Of course he may. And while the hotel staff scurry backwards and forwards attending to his needs, the porter obligingly pores over the local *What's On* on his behalf. 'Can you recommend a good film? Who's in it? Who's the director? What time does the show begin? What time does the show end?'

Evidently deciding against taking in a movie, he then goes for a stroll, badgering total strangers for information about his surroundings: 'What's that building? Who was the architect? Who built it? When did he live? When was it built?' Surprisingly, this hectoring technique seems to win him friends, for soon he is exchanging pleasantries: 'How do you do? How are you?'

With his new friends, he goes for dinner. Whether he is anxious to make an impression on them we are not told, but it appears that the restaurant fails to meet his exacting standards. 'That's not what I ordered. The meat is overdone, underdone, too tough. This is too bitter, sour, salty, sweet. The food is cold. What's taking you so long? This isn't clean. Where are our drinks?'

After this disappointing experience our intrepid explorer returns to his hotel – now, to his disillusioned eye, to be revealed as the back-street dump it really is. 'The air conditioning doesn't work. The wash-basin is clogged. The window is jammed. The blind is stuck. These aren't my shoes. This isn't my laundry. Where is the socket for my razor? I've lost my watch. The lamp is broken. The room is too noisy. There are no towels. There is no plug. There is no toilet paper. *I want to stay another night.*'

Perhaps we should get the car out and give those cassettes another whirl. Meanwhile we may take comfort from the knowledge that English is the international language of airports, terrorists, graffitists, pornographers, tourist traps, hotel receptionists and head porters, some waiters and fewer taxi drivers.

Menu-lingual

But while phrase books are best read as literature, a trusty lexicon for use in restaurants is essential. I have stuck to that view ever since, when scanning a Bavarian dinner menu thirty-odd years ago, I asked for the printer in the belief that he was a dish of mixed vegetables.

While most tourist menus offer an English translation ('Escalope of weal mit primacy of the saison'), the classier establishments and those interesting little places off the beaten track very often do not. Failing the company of an interpreter, I always carry a menu guide with me. In Europe, I use a little volume called *The Instant Menu Translator*, published by Foulsham, which briefs the innocent diner in French, German, Italian and Spanish.

It is a very simple little handbook. Say you fancy

the *Rote Ruben*: before setting your taste-buds a-tingling in expectation of a nice hot Reuben sandwich you look up the appropriate entry under the appropriate language to learn that you were on the verge of ordering a dish of beetroot.

I find ordinary translation dictionaries worse than useless in restaurants. We may, by plodding through a pocket German–English/English–German dictionary, be able to work out that *Pökelrinderbrust* is salt cattle chest, but is it the same kind of salt cattle chest we are accustomed to ordering at home? It needs a specialist menu dictionary to tell us that it is 'usually a very tender, mild and juicy piece of boiled pickled beef, delicious when washed down with a mug of beer'. Again, in the case of finding Macedonia under *dolci*, it may be the work of a moment, should we happen to be carrying volume 14 of the *Encyclopaedia Britannica* around with us, to ascertain that Macedonia is the central part of the Balkan peninsula, strategically important as a crossroads to both the Roman and Ottoman Empires, with a total population in 1961 of 1,404,883; but we should fail to learn that as a pudding course, Macedonia is less of a Balkan peninsula and more of a fresh fruit salad with maraschino liqueur.

In the absence of a menu translator or an English-speaking waiter, and in countries where the language is not so much unfamiliar as incomprehensible, I tend – particularly if we are in sheep's eyeball territory – to play safe and point to what someone else is having. Not that this is a foolproof way of ordering a meal. Long, long ago, in Naples on one of my first foreign trips, I confidently instructed the waiter, 'My guest will have the cheese, and for dessert I think I'll have that ice-creamy-looking dish that chap over there is eating.'

'Is mozzarella, sair. *Formaggio*. Cheese.'

'OK, my guest will have the cheese, and for dessert I'll have some of that cheese.'

Sights

Dr Johnson had a poor opinion of sightseers. He described the typical pilgrim of the Grand Tour as 'one who enters a town at night and surveys it in the morning, and then hastens away to another place . . . with a confused remembrance of palaces and churches.'

He also said, 'There are some things to see and there are some things to go to see.' Travellers see, tourists go to see. Hence Malcolm Muggeridge spent six years in India and never saw the Taj Mahal nor had any wish to see it, while his wife lived two years in Cairo without ever going out to the Pyramids.

I confess myself an inveterate sightseer. If there is a famous tomb, a monument, an ancient ruin, a wonder of the world within a fifty-mile radius of where I am, I will go out and stare at it. But Sam Johnson had it right. With the exception of some of the great historical set pieces like Pompeii or Williamsburg or the Valley of the Kings where you do feel you're absorbing something of the feel and purpose of a place, the experience of visiting a Lenin's Tomb or Statue of Liberty or Sydney Opera House is curiously deadening. One brings nothing away from it except that confused remembrance that Johnson speaks of. I carry far sharper and far more fruitful memories of some of the famous pictures I have seen, the favourites I will go to gaze at over and over again without ever thinking, 'Right, so that's Van Gogh crossed off the list.'

On the Grand Tour, you were expected to sketch everything in sight. Now, you're expected to photograph everything in sight. When it comes to dulled senses the camera has a lot to answer for: there is no fabulous sight on earth that photography has not over-familiarised us with before we ever set eyes on it in the flesh. Among my favourite pictures is not the Mona Lisa, who suffers from over-exposure.

What is more, that third eye which we hang around our necks stops the other two from seeing anything worthwhile. Taking in my first sight of the Grand Canyon a few summers ago, I watched a party of Japanese tourists troop out of their coach, already raising their cameras and squinting through their viewfinders as they crossed the car lot. They approached the great crater and took numerous pictures of it, and of one another standing on the rim. (The average Japanese tourist gets through six rolls of film a day, I'm told.) They then, without a further glance at one of the most awesome spectacles on earth (well, it is to me: others have likened it to a big quarry), headed back for their coach and were whisked away, doubtless to pose for the camera arm-in-arm with a cactus in the Petrified Forest.

But it is not for me to cast the first stone at the snap-happy, much though I should like to when expected by some pushy lens-twiddler to move off the *palazzo* steps so that he can take a picture of his wife licking an ice-cream on them. There is hardly a tourist attraction in the world that I have not photographed, or been myself photographed standing in front of or under or on top of. But even with the pictorial record there before my eyes in glorious Eastman colour, remembrance is still confused. Is that the Eiffel Tower or Blackpool Tower? Is this one Herculaneum or Rome? Far too late in life, I learned to start captioning my photographs the moment they were back from the developers. After a year or two, one beach, one Roman ruin, one colonnade, one pavement café, looks much like another.

While I remain a pushover for sights, I do these days make a point of not taking their photographs. I find I can see much better without a camera. It is also far more relaxing to wander around just getting the feel of a place without endlessly looking for photo-opportunities.

Photography and flight between them moulded the character of modern tourism. The wide-bodied jet enables us to travel great distances at comparatively low cost. The Instamatic camera enables us to take a snap of the Golden Gate Bridge the moment we get there. Of the two, possibly photography is the greater influence – the more photogenic the resort, the more popular it is. Without flight, there would still be mass travel, with package tours crammed into boats and trains instead of aeroplanes. Without cameras, tourists would not know what on earth to do with their hands. Perhaps they would take to carrying walking sticks – but that would make them travellers.

I cannot imagine why anyone should want to go into a gallery or museum and (usually against the rules) take a picture of a picture, when they can go down to the shop in the lobby and buy a perfectly good reproduction on a postcard. Perhaps galleries and museums bore them and they are just passing the time. Many worthy folk who do not set foot in the British Museum or the Tate or the National Gallery from one year's end to the next will make a point of doing the rounds of the museums when they are on foreign soil. My guess is that when they arrive to find the museum closed, as it frequently is, they are secretly relieved. But should they, to their chagrin, find it open, they will spend far too much time trailing round it out of a sense of duty. Hunter Davies wrote in *Punch*, 'I love museums and visit them frequently. But my engagement span is seventeen minutes. I suspect many people are much the same.' So do I. See what you've come to see, but where's the point of staring at case after case of bits of broken terracotta, just to assuage a feeling of guilt at not really being much of a one for antiquities?

The ideal traveller is a temperate man, with a sound constitution, a digestion like an ostrich, a good temper, and no race prejudice.

WILLIAM HENRY CROSSE
Medical Hints, 1906

Ten Things a Bright Tourist Can Do

Unless you are a dedicated sun-worshipper, in which case I shall leave you to your own devices, you are bound to have a good deal of spare time on holiday. That, after all, is what you are there to enjoy. By spare time I mean what is left over between mealtimes and bouts of sightseeing. It is tempting to fritter away these odd hours on mooching about or sitting around in cafés, and indeed a goodly proportion of them should be so frittered. But it is easy to tip the balance and find yourself reduced to hanging around the hotel lounge watching bicycle races on television, or walking aimlessly about stores indistinguishable from Habitat and Next. This is where relaxing ends and inertia begins.

While it would be self-defeating to exhaust yourself on holiday, it generates a feeling of well-being to keep busy, or anyway persuade yourself that you're keeping busy, by arranging it so that each day seems agreeably crammed with activity. The secret is to assign yourself little tasks and errands to occupy the spare hour before the coach leaves for the tour of the wine region with lunch at a sixteenth-century château, and even more importantly the longest hour of the day which is when you've had all the aperitifs you can take and it's still nowhere near dinner-time. These are some of the ways in which diligent tourists may occupy themselves:

Tracking down the English papers and pinpointing their approximate (wildly approximate, it will turn out) time of arrival; whereafter, having worked out that you have paid the equivalent of three pounds for yesterday's *Times*, trying to get that amount's worth of reading out of it over a cup of coffee costing just about the same. NB: Resign yourself to the fact that there is always one day of the week when the papers inexplicably fail to arrive.

Traipsing round the market and comparing the price of fruit, veg, cheese, eggs, live hens etc there with the price of the same produce here, except for the live hens. Since the calculations involved are in the order of, 'Half a kilo, call that just over a pound –

fifteen hundred lire, say that's about sixty pee,' the exercise is not very enlightening, but it passes the morning and you do meet a good class of fruit and veg.

Buying stamps. This is a major enterprise. The hotel has run out of them, the kiosk that supplied the postcards does not supply stamps, you cannot find the post office (it is the building with two cigarette-puffing guards in dark glasses lounging under the national flag), and when you do find it, it is closed because today is a government holiday. Persevere, and ultimately you will progress beyond the threshold, where you will behold what looks like a busy railway booking-hall with many queues, but only one of them, it yet remains to be discovered by trial and error, for stamps. Hours of fun for all the family.

Writing postcards. On the postcard front, travellers divide themselves into four categories – those who never send them at all; those who punctiliously despatch them the day after they arrive; those who put it off until the very last minute so that they get back home ahead of their own 'Wish you were here'; and the great majority who scribble their cards at odd moments, usually while waiting for their partners to get ready to go out. This is all very well and it gives one something to do instead of pacing up and down the hotel lobby fuming, but it deprives one of the real satisfaction of a job well done which is to be derived from sitting down at a café table with address book and batch of cards, and ploughing through them until the chore is finished. As to what to write on them beyond the conventionalities, I am afraid I am no use, since for years I have been in the first category. Although I have earned my living by my pen all my life, you have only to put a picture postcard in front of me and tell me to think up fifty words to put on it, and my mind goes blank.

Changing money. Not at the hotel, which will not only give you a worse rate even than the *bureaux de change*, but will make the experience a disappointingly smooth, unforeign one. Go instead to one of the national banks of the country. Like the post office, it is more likely to be closed than not; but should you gain admittance you can happily spend a morning being shuffled from one counter to another and enjoying the satisfactory thud of rubber stamps on forms made out in quintuplicate. Marvel at a bureaucracy that makes ours look like casual informality. Don't forget your passport, which they will want to examine several times before you get your money.

Toothpaste expeditions. If you have followed the advice under *Packing*, you are going to run out of toothpaste, razor blades, Alka-Seltzer or whatever before your holiday is over. This gives you a positive task and an absorbing one, since many of these ordinary commodities are often extraordinarily difficult to find. The chemist, it turns out (that's when you've finally located a chemist) does not sell film, nor does the newspaper kiosk sell matches. You could bring the search to an abrupt end by heading for some store like Uniprix which will sell you anything you want, but that would bring the enjoyment of the chase to an end too.

Looking for restaurants. Many countries require their eating houses to post their menus outside where prospective customers can inspect the prices before going in (so do we, come to that, but the regulation is commonly ignored). In other countries the custom is usually observed anyway. Thus, armed with *Michelin*, you have the appetite-whetting opportunity to stroll from restaurant to restaurant, comparing cuisine and cost and checking out the ambience. (As to how to track down just the right place, refer to my *Theory & Practice of Lunch*.) If it looks like the kind of restaurant where it would be wise to book, pop in and do so. It is amazing how many Brits abroad are to be seen wandering hungrily about in circles come dinner-time, not having rumbled that the locals like to eat out too and are apt, quite rightly, to hog the best restaurants.

Planning excursions. The easiest and most boring way to arrange your half-day city tour or outing to the Roman villa is to pick up a few leaflets at your hotel, make your choice, and get the concierge to fix it. The more purposeful way is to proceed to the tour office where you may find a wider choice of excursions (some hotels only book the tours that pick up at their own doors). Once you have made your choice, over something cool at the pavement café next door, you can while away a pleasant half-hour behind a middle-aged couple who have got as far as the ticket counter without being able to agree where they want to go, and who are now looking to the clerk to arbitrate. Your recompense for any exasperation generated is a feeling of smug achievement at having gone out and adventurously arranged something for yourself.

Buying presents. The temptation is to do this in dribs and drabs, picking up a peasant's shawl here and a hand-decorated pair of wooden shoes there. It is far more satisfying to put aside a whole morning for present-buying, rewarding yourself with a slap-up lunch when all is in hand. If you think half a day too long for this agreeable task, don't forget that the lace shop where you spotted just the thing for Mother earlier in the week is likely to have vanished off the face of the earth when you come to look for it. NB: But before buying anything, turn to *Among Your Souvenirs*.

Getting orientated. All the above tasks will be that much easier to accomplish if you get through this last one first. Having acquired a map and made sure you are holding it the right way up, familiarise yourself with the locality by taking a circuitous tour from your hotel, establishing landmarks ('Now remember, to get to the fish market we have to turn right at that flower stall') so that on future jaunts you will know for certain that you are going the wrong way. As for turning right at the flower stall, how were you to know that it is identical to another flower stall, turning right at which will lead you to the gasworks?

Among Your Souvenirs

Everyone knows that wire coathangers multiply like rabbits. What is not so generally known is that holiday souvenirs self-destruct like lemmings. Otherwise where are they all?

How often have you not been able to get on the airport bus for camel saddles? Yet how often have you sat on a camel saddle in someone's home? When last did you stub out a cigarette on a souvenir ashtray?

Consider. The resort of Taramasalata, frequented exclusively by the British, boasts a hundred souvenir shops. The speciality of the region is a musical box fashioned out of local plastic and decorated with imported seashells, which plays 'It's a Long Way to Taramasalata'. Let us say that each shop sells a hundred of these trinkets per day, seven days a week.

That is nearly two million musical boxes per season. Thus, since the tourist industry got into its stride in the Fifties, there must have built up a musical box mountain sufficient to provide one of these tinkling toys to every man, woman and child in the country. Yet the only way you will ever get to see or hear one is by going back to Taramasalata.

Do they, then, vanish into a musical box Sargasso Sea where if you lift a conch-shell to your ears it plays 'Come Back to Sorrento' or 'Wonderful, Wonderful Copenhagen'? No: unlike the souvenirs of bygone days which called themselves 'A Trifle From Margate' and which can now be snapped up in antique shops for a trifling number of tenners, modern souvenirs have built-in obsolescence. Shortly after your reproduction mock-Benaresware miniature dinner gong has been carted a couple of thousand miles homeward, presented to Auntie Maude and given pride of place on top of the piano where the wire Sicilian donkey cart used to be, a process of rapid disintegration sets in. Soon, it will have melted away like a souvenir icicle ('A Present From Iceland') to make way for a model of the Acropolis in simulated alabaster.

These days I rarely bring anything back from abroad except wine and food. That goes missing at once too, but I do know where it's gone. I never was much of a one for souvenirs and as for local artefacts, unless you get your suits made in Hong Kong or your silk dresses in Bangkok, or you have a penchant for fake Rolex Oysters, there is very little in our global village market nowadays that cannot be bought everywhere else. Among items I particularly don't bring back are the following:

> Maximum seven litres of duty-frees which grow heavier with every clanking step, and which are apt to finish up as a heap of broken glass on Heathrow tube station when the carrier bag handles snap;
> Paperweights in the shape of any building or edifice;
> Any object which lights up or plays tunes;
> All Italian leather stamped with Prince of Wales feathers or representations of amphitheatres;
> Neat kitchen gadgets from Uniprix which are never going to be used;
> Murano glass that looks as if it came from Woolworth's the moment it's unpacked;
> French coffee cups which can be easily bought at David Mellor;
> Biscuit tins that look like the Taj Mahal;
> Liqueurs contained in any bottle which is not bottle-shaped;
> Cheeses which pass their sell-by date half-way across the Channel;
> Dolls wearing national costume;
> Hats which draw attention to themselves;
> Anything that has to be carried as hand-baggage and which proclaims its origins (or rather its purported origins, since it was probably made in Taiwan) such as boomerangs, wooden garden forks as used by Spanish peasants, and African carvings;
> Objets d' folk art.

Hats which draw attention to themselves . . .

If you are hellbent on coming home laden with mementoes, there are a few golden rules for the discerning traveller. Never buy anything from a souvenir shop. If it is not trash it will be overpriced. Use the shops the locals use and you will get your cotton goods or sponges or leather at half the price. Buy only local products. There is little point in buying peasant dolls made in China, unless you happen to be in China at the time of purchase. Stuff imported to the mainland from a nearby island always costs more – go to the island itself, and have a

111

pleasant outing into the bargain. Finally, the simpler the artefact, the more likely it is to give pleasure and to be a real memento of its original habitat. Cigarette boxes encrusted with sea shells evoke memories only of sitting about in a hot and crowded airport.

We all know this hotel in which we can get anything we want, after its kind, for money; but where nobody is glad to see us, or sorry to see us, or minds (our bill paid) whether we come or go . . . We all know that we can get on very well indeed at such a place, but still not perfectly well; and this may be, because the place is largely wholesale, and there is a lingering personal retail interest within us that asks us to be satisfied.

CHARLES DICKENS

EXCESS
BAGGAGE

Impulse Flying

*A*rmchair travelling notwithstanding, there is nothing so exhilarating as throwing some things in a bag and taking off at a couple of days' or even a couple of minutes' notice. Living in Brighton as I do, I can look out of my window at 6.30 a.m., decide it's a nice day, and within half an hour be on the seven o'clock ferry from Newhaven, arriving in Dieppe just in time to spring across to La Moderne restaurant for a fishy lunch. Loaded with wine and cheese and smelling somewhat of cognac, I am back the same evening with an air of well-being which on more formally-planned jaunts would take a week to acquire.

I could just as easily hop on a train to Gatwick and take the next plane out to Paris. In this country, we have not yet got hold of the idea of using airports like bus stations, as the Americans do. It is, should the fit take you, perfectly feasible to sit down to breakfast with no thought in your head of going to Rome, yet to be dining on the Piazza Navona that evening. You simply ring the airline and book a ticket, paying for it at the airport. Buy currency at the airport branch of your bank, having no truck with High Street *bureaux de change* who are often usurers. You either ring a hotel and book a room before you set off (they'll confirm it in exchange for a credit card number) or if you don't have the appropriate *Michelin* handy (why not?) call one of the chain hotels here and get them to make the booking for you, or if you don't want to stay in an international hotel or it's too pricey, get a travel agent to help – just so long as you don't run out of time and put the trip off till tomorrow or next week.

Otherwise, and this is the move I recommend, you just set off and find somewhere to stay when you get there. If you can't get yourself fixed up at the airport, where there are usually hotel phones and probably an accommodation enquiry desk, go to the tourist office, or if that's closed use my favoured method, which is simply to arrive at the hotel of my choice and if there's no room at the inn, throw myself on their mercy. Hotels are remarkably good about finding rooms with their rivals for total strangers – I suppose they regard it as bread cast upon the waters. Even at the busiest times there are always rooms to be found somewhere. I've arrived in Munich in the middle of the Bierfest, Nice just in time for the Battle of Flowers, San Francisco at the start of a Democratic convention, New Orleans at the start of a Republican one, and Accra on the eve of Ghana's independence day celebrations, and never had to sleep on a park bench. You may end up in a side street but that's part of the adventure – and aren't those Hamelinesque terracotta rooftops enchanting?

I forgot to say that that air ticket you bought should have been a return one, but if it isn't I'm sure you can get back home somehow. The essence of impulse flying is that you are doing it by the seat of your pants, and whatever element of uncertainty it entails adds a few bubbles to the euphoria of finding yourself on the Boulevard Montparnasse when you thought you'd be doing the gardening.

Half-way between armchair travelling and impulse flying, and a compromise for those who really do like or need a bit of notice before taking off, is the forwardly-planned whim, where instead of going on the spur of the moment you leave on the spur of next week. There are all manner of mini-break deals you can arrange at a few days' notice through a travel agent, or you can put your own package together, following pretty well the same procedure as for impulse flying. Which brings us to —

Le Weekend

A weekend is a long time on holiday. But in contrast to that week which is a long time in politics, it is more than likely to be a lot of fun.

It would need an Einstein to explain this, but the shorter the period away from home, the longer it feels, and the further abroad one ventures, the more one seems to have been gone for weeks on end –

except in retrospect when you step out of your jet-engined time machine to find only a couple of circulars on the mat and no messages on the answering machine. To travel from Friday to Sunday is to have arrived and come back before the neighbours even notice you're gone.

I am a dedicated snatcher of holiday weekends, preferring them, indeed, to set-piece summer fortnights. They can be taken at short notice as the need and opportunity arise. They induce none of the trepidation with which one faces longer hauls, since what may be sheer hell on a major holiday turned sour – bad weather, awful room, frightful food – is but lighthearted anecdotal purgatory when you know there's only forty-eight hours of it. They pep up the system, refresh the parts a weekend's golf or gardening cannot reach, and replenish the wine-rack with duty-frees – all without having to squander any of those precious squares on the office holiday roster.

The away-weekend, in essence, is organised truancy – a form of more-or-less sanctioned hookey when there's no time for a proper holiday or when you feel you've earned a mid-term prize between one chunk of work and the next. Or – but why look for excuses? The best weekend holiday is (see *Impulse Flying*) when you suddenly decide to take off to heaven for the hell of it.

But there's more to it than chucking a few things in a suitcase and hoping for the best. It has to be a planned operation – which is no great chore, since planning holidays is almost as agreeable as having them.

What Dr Johnson said about the imminent prospect of being hanged, that it concentrates the mind wonderfully, could equally be said of the mini-break where even if you send off your postcards the moment you get there, you are going to be home again before they arrive.

No time for that first leisurely recce of the town, for putting off till tomorrow the perusing of the guide book that will tell you the museum isn't open till the day after, for browsing round the wine shop without buying, for mooching around looking at menus.

Everything has to be done now – and everything has to be done right. Tonight's dinner, tomorrow's lunch, must be memorable experiences – you do not, on so short a flight from the cares of the humdrum day, want to finish up in a back-street pizza joint because you couldn't find the restaurant a friend recommended and the other one that looked a likely place is full.

So there has to be organisation and homework – maps, guides, itineraries, restaurant lists, all marshalled and assimilated before you set off. And while you needn't draw up a rigid programme, you have to decide what's feasible and what isn't. The beauty spot 150 kilometres away is out. So are two out of a possible three museums or galleries. You can wander around the market on Saturday morning or you can do the ducal palace, but you cannot do both. (Do the market.)

Ideally, the holiday weekend should resemble the weekend bag you take with you. It should contain everything you need and a few things you don't, but it should not be so jam-packed that there's no room for some last-minute frippery.

Not that a holiday weekend has to serve any purpose other than perking one up and making one's friends jealous, but it does have one practical use, and that is to act as a taster for longer holidays. Should you decide that the place is worth a return visit you will more or less know your way around. And you'll be able to do all the things you couldn't fit in before – the market *and* the ducal palace.

Have a good weekend.

A traveller has a right to relate and embellish his adventures as he pleases, and it is very impolite to refuse that deference and applause they deserve.

RUDOLF ERICH RASPE
Travels of Baron Munchausen

Le Dirty Weekend

A Brighton hotel manager estimated – or perhaps he got it off his computer – that eighty per cent of couples sampling his winter-break discount week-ends are in bed within an hour of checking in.

. . . **in bed within an hour of checking in**

While it does not follow that they must all be unmarried, the statistic is a strong indicator that the dirty weekend is alive and well and still living in Brighton.

Like the hotels that play host to them, dirty weekends have undergone some refurbishment over the years. It is no longer necessary to sign in as Mr and Mrs Smith, or to over-tip the saucy chambermaid who has noticed that madam isn't wearing a wedding ring. That man unnervingly peering over his newspaper, who seems to be a permanent fixture of the lobby, is no longer likely to be a private detective. The dirty weekend itself, these days, is a movable feast, being as often as not a dirty Wednesday or other weekday when it is easier for erring husbands (and erring wives) to get away. As often as not, by the same token, the institution often goes under the alias of business conference.

But some aspects of the dirty weekend, unlike its participants, remain constant. The likelihood of bumping into someone you know, for instance, is as high as it ever was – indeed, in these mobile days, it is getting higher all the time, and it seems to be a rule that the more improbable and inaccessible the venue, the likelier it is that you will be spotted. A couple I know, in the course of an office liaison, hid themselves away in the remotest pub they could find, high up in the Yorkshire Dales. Coming down dishevelled to refresh themselves on real ale, they found the sole occupant of the snug to be their sales director, drinking champagne, this being his home village. (The record for being recognised the furthest away from home is held by another pair I know who, trudging round a department store in some far-flung province of China, were hailed by someone who proved to be the *maître d'* of their local Chinese restaurant in Ealing, who happened to be visiting his family.)

The possibility of an emergency arising at home during your absence also remains a fair to certain chance. This means that you had better be where you said you were going. And while reception has known all along that your companion is not your legal spouse, when you're handed a message slip asking you to ring your wife or husband, you must be prepared for smirks. The smirks, indeed, may have been passing to and fro across the front desk since your arrival. Where the dirty weekend is staggered into the working week, the hotel is most likely to have been booked through the office, thus it is one person they are expecting, not one plus, even though you may have specified a double room to work in (you didn't care to specify a double bed to work on). Flickering an up-and-down glance at your companion who is studiously examining the dining room menu some feet away, the receptionist regards your unmatching luggage and enquires, with laid-back courtesy, 'And it's double occupancy is it, sir?' The manner is cool but the innuendo is in the same league as the narrowed eyes of the suspicious Blackpool boarding-house keeper back in the era of *Hindle Wakes*.

So all in all, despite the morally relaxed times we still live in even though it cannot be long now before every business class air ticket carries a Government AIDS warning, the dirty weekend can be as fraught an experience as it ever was. It is therefore not a bad idea to take some precautions beyond the obvious ones.

Try to arrange your tryst at some venue where eyebrows will not be raised should you be seen together. The more obvious the rendezvous, the less you will arouse suspicions – or anyway, suspicions that can be substantiated. If you are both in the same way of business, then conferences, fairs, seminars and whatnot present ideal opportunities. If not, then this advice is perhaps more easily given than taken (though statistics prove, I shouldn't wonder, that couples on this sort of jaunt often do have something professionally, as well as personally, in common). But at least, in that case, don't travel together. Airports and railway stations are where you are most likely to be seen.

If you must travel in tandem, don't do it on the same ticket or voucher. This is less to do with evidence for the divorce lawyer than with the fact that it sometimes turns out on dirty weekends that the couple who arrive together have not the slightest desire to leave together, nor indeed to see one another ever again. Separate tickets mean you can return to your separate beds and separate lives with the minimum of heavy sighs and sulks.

Like newlyweds, dirty weekenders tend to set off in such a state of agitation that disappointment is almost inevitable unless they allow for its possibility.

A sound principle is, if not to expect the worst, then certainly not to anticipate the best. High expectations do not sit well with nagging anxiety. The routine frustrations of hotel life – the bed not made up after lunch, room service tardy, the bathroom light not working – tend to blow themselves up out of all proportion when you have been desperately banking on everything going smoothly.

The person most likely to receive an unexpected phone call in the middle of the night should make a point of sleeping next to the telephone. Being forbidden to pick up the phone for fear it is your bedmate's partner/boss/babysitter is bad enough – automatically answering it while half-asleep is disaster.

Have no truck with any hotel offering Romantic Weekends with champagne, candle-lit dinners and a red rose on your pillow. The place will be packed with married couples enjoying a second honeymoon and you will feel wretched and guilty.

Finally, it is in no spirit of prudery that I raise the question you should be asking yourself in the first place – is your journey really necessary? As I have already noted, a weekend is a long time on holiday. With someone you don't know very well, it can be an eternity.

The man who goes alone can start today; but he who travels with another must wait till that other is ready.

HENRY DAVID THOREAU

In Defence of Holiday Romances

A woman of my acquaintance fell in love with a gondolier on one of those moonlight serenades they have along the Grand Canal. She moved permanently to Venice, learned Italian and married him; and to the best of my knowledge they have lived happily ever after.

Is she the exception that proves the rule? Do all holiday romances come to nothing – or worse, to grief? Why do they have such a bad name?

Agony aunties must take most of the blame. Moist-eyed typists back from the Costa del Chat-up are forever soliciting advice on what is to be done about the olive-eyed beach boys who wooed and won them, who promised on that last magic evening to write with the precise date on which they expected to arrive on these shores to find jobs as waiters in order to be near the one who taught them the meaning of the verb to love, but who have unaccountably not been heard from since.

The counsel these lovelorn maidens – correction, lovelorn ladies – invariably get is, 'Look, love, you've had your holiday fling – now forget him, because, let's face it, he's already forgotten you and you can bet your bottom drawer he is in somebody else's arms by now.'

This is probably true, but is it necessarily true? Who is to say that the beach boy's letter was not lost in the post, or that he did not get the address wrong and send it, in his swooning preoccupation, to Dunroamin, Ecstasy Avenue instead of Dunroamin, Acacia Avenue, or that his sizzling message did not get wedged in the pillar box to be eaten by snails?

It is a very curious truth that people strike up love affairs all over the place – in the office, the disco, the pub, at parties – and nobody minds, yet as soon as they fall in love on a stretch of sand against a background of waving palms, they are derided. Best friends who look forward to being bridesmaids when the last of their number to remain single seems thoroughly besotted with that portly, middle-aged jute importer she met at the Chamber of Commerce annual dinner dance, will roll their eyes and ask one another rhetorically when she will ever learn when they hear that she has fallen for a sun-bronzed young blade encountered over an exotic drink served in a scooped-out pineapple on that Caribbean jaunt her parents took her on.

Theory has it that love has got to pass all sorts of tests before it is awarded the seal of approval as the Real Thing. You have to remain in love on rainy days as well as on sunny ones, in fits of gloom and despondency as well as in bouts of euphoria, in sickness as well as in health.

Very possibly. But where all the holiday romance cynics go wrong is in assuming that because a serious relationship is not in itself one long holiday, it should not be contracted into while on one. This pre-supposes that passionate commitments entered into outside the heady influence of the moonlight shimmering over the Mediterranean will have commenced in an atmosphere of sense and sensibility – which is manifestly not true. I know a girl who met, married and had children by a wrong number on her telephone.

Earls, we all know, once had a healthy reputation for marrying chorus girls. Then why shouldn't commoners marry beach boys – or, for that matter, earls marry chalet girls?

There may be, it has to be conceded, language problems. If you cannot get your partner to comprehend that you wish to be passed the salt, the marriage may be heading for the rocks. But if two people, being of sound mind and body, should fall in love in a romantic setting while in a relaxed frame of mind, and they are able to understand one another, then I see no reason why they are reckoned to have less chance of lasting happiness than the couple I know, now approaching their silver wedding, who became acquainted while waiting on the same street corner for a taxi.

It is popularly supposed that travellers of the female persuasion are more susceptible to the allegedly fatal lure of the holiday romance. I don't know about that: British men go abroad in the same

Why on earth shouldn't a nice well brought up English girl fall in love with a foreign waiter?

quantity as British women and, if single, presumably with the same intention; it is just that we hear less about the consequences, or lack of them. They tend not to write to the agony aunts complaining that the *señorita* of their dreams has failed to fulfil her pledge to follow them to the ends of the earth, or anyway the ends of Cricklewood.

Another accusation laid at the door of holiday romances is that the lithe, medallioned Romeos who haunt the beaches have such a terrible line in chat, with a tendency to compare the eyes of their conquests with anything wet – lakes, mountain pools, the Med etc. But this is surely not because they are frauds but because they are foreign. An Italian computer salesman, in the course of attempting to win the heart of his female opposite number at an international software exhibition in Slough, would make a similar comparison. It is simply the way they talk.

Observing holiday romantics on my frequent trips abroad, and noting what a thoroughly good time they seem to have while progressing from shyly identifying their soulmates at some café table or poolside to adoringly shovelling forkfuls of seafood into one another's mouths in a lantern-lit open-air restaurant with a musical instrument of some kind playing softly in the background, I wonder how anyone could possibly think they would be wiser to stay indoors swotting up the next day's itinerary in the guide book.

Here's to holiday romances – and why on earth shouldn't a nice, well-brought-up British girl fall in love with a foreign waiter? She might finish up running a restaurant.

What Holiday?

The best place to be on a public holiday is at home with a six-pack, watching the ferry queues at Dover on TV.

I chance to be writing this passage on a Good Friday. Should I experience any pang of self-pity at working while a goodly proportion of the western world is not, I need only turn to the morning's papers:

'Holiday chaos as roads are jammed solid . . . Easter holidaymakers attempting to make an early start faced appalling traffic conditions . . . Described by police as "streaming out of the cities like lemmings", thousands of drivers found themselves in traffic jams as early as midday. For three hours traffic on the M1 was at a virtual standstill for thirty miles between Watford and Northampton, and there was a ten-mile tailback at the Dartford Tunnel. The volume of information received at the AA's Roadwatch headquarters was so vast that its computer lost its memory and was out of action for most of the day . . .

'Meanwhile the strike by P & O seamen at Dover means that none of the firm's British-crewed ships is sailing from Dover to Calais. "Unless you have a firm reservation, don't attempt to travel," advised a spokesman. No more P & O bookings are now being taken until two days after Easter for Dover to Ostend, Portsmouth to Le Havre and Cherbourg, or Felixstowe to Zeebrugge.

'At Gatwick, Easter began with baggage-hall problems due to a new staff shift system. About 800 passengers had to wait for nearly two hours to reclaim their luggage. At Heathrow, with 112,000 expected to fly out over Easter, terminals were jammed . . .'

That, as anyone foolhardy enough to join in the holiday stampede will testify, is a fair profile of the Easter break. It is almost as bad in August, and give or take a few degrees of bedlam, on all the other public holidays. Instead of the travel agents wringing their hands and complaining that they have never been busier (they are much like farmers in looking their gift horses in the mouth), they would do well to blow up these holiday chaos reports to poster size and plaster their windows with them as a deterrent to potential travellers.

Why do we do it? Because memory fades and time heals, I suppose: and because it is easy to persuade ourselves that last year was exceptional – the ferrymen were on strike, there were cone-laying operations on the motorway, the baggage handlers were working to rule, there were teething troubles at the new terminal. . . . But the point is that there is no such thing as a one-off hitch in bank holiday travel arrangements. The snags recur like bad dreams. If there is no ferry strike, then there will be an air traffic controllers' strike. If the baggage handlers are not working to rule, then the customs men will be working to rule. If there were no delays on the M1 – but there we are straying into a travelogue world of fantasy. There will always be bank holiday chaos because bank holidays generate chaos, and there is never going to be a year when the papers miraculously report, 'Holiday calm as roads are reasonably quiet . . .' There is not enough road, not enough air space, not enough boats, to accommodate the numbers who want to get away.

For many travellers, it's a choice between taking a break over the bank holiday weekend or not taking one at all. For those in a position to be more flexible, the golden rule should be: whatever you do at holiday time, don't go on holiday.

Must We Take the Children?

Let us be blunt about this. Are your children reasonably well-behaved? If not, or they are hyperactive or sometimes apt to get a little overexcited if you want to put it that way, then they are going to be a pain in the neck both to you and your fellow-guests. But against that, travel is one of the great civilising influences. Children regularly exposed to it, like children taken to restaurants from an early age, gradually assimilate the social confidence and good manners of their elders and betters. So what we have here is a chicken and egg situation.

Other things being equal, and tantrums being kept down to the minimum, it comes down largely to the age at which the child starts being trundled about. I have to say from the start that I am against boiling babies. It is a cruel thing to expose a babe in arms to unaccustomed sun, and a cruel act against all exposed to its yelling in the night, including its harassed parents, one of whom is to be observed long after the dinner hour still morosely toying with an aperitif and doing yesterday's *Times* crossword while the other one tries to get the wretched child down. Tiny children can be a thundering nuisance on aircraft, too. 'Try flying with a baby if you want a sense of what it must have been like to be a leper in the 14th century,' wrote Nora Ephron. Point taken: but try flying next to someone else's baby on the long haul from Honolulu if you want a sense of appreciation of just how peaceful the 14th century must have been.

If tiny children can't be left with Granny, they are better conveyed by car and decanted into a rented villa. Villa addicts are a particular breed and will not need me to point out the hazards of getting there (drafters of directions have a habit of instructing, 'turn left on narrow dirt track before piggery' without indicating how you are supposed to figure out that you are approaching the piggery. Perhaps by the smell?); the complex plumbing arrangements ('To flush, draw plunger and press, but not too smartly'); or the tendency for all the lights to go off when you finally work out how to switch on the table lamps. Those not well-versed in villas should turn to John Mortimer's novel, *Summer's Lease*, before coming to any firm decision.

Flying next to someone else's baby

But I contend that children do not need holidays until they are four (life is one long holiday until nursery school), and that they cannot begin to appreciate foreign holidays until they are at least nine. My own brood holidayed each year in Cornwall, in family hotels where there were plenty of other children to play with, until the youngest of them was nine, when they started being taken abroad, starting cautiously with St Malo and ending the cycle at San Francisco, by which time they were all grown up and one of my daughters was setting off for a year-long trek around the world.

Until they have reached an age where architecture no longer bores them and they are capable of sitting still at a restaurant table while the adults finish their coffee, children need plenty to do on holiday. You cannot blame them for finding grown-up preoccupations boring (though I draw the line at the little wretch I overheard complaining, 'There's nothing to do in Kenya'), and after all it is easy enough to find something a little more stimulating for them to pass the time than bouncing a beachball down the hotel stairs. Getting together the ingredients for a picnic, with the children allowed to roam through the market on their own, each with a specific errand, is always good fun, so long as they are old enough to be let off the leash and are adequately labelled. So are independent shopping expeditions for postcards or Granny's present, if it is sufficiently drummed into them that they are not allowed to stray out of view of your café table, and that if they step into the road they are going to be flattened by a corrugated tin car. As for the sights, castles and ruins, if climbable, always go down well, as do dungeons and torture chambers, city walls, boats landing the fishing catch, anywhere where the people wear funny clothes, and of course beaches, especially those with rocky pools suitable for shrimping and falling in, or with the potential for collecting shells or sting-rays.

All children love camping holidays and here again they like to be assigned tasks such as fetching the bread or feeding radishes to the goat. I haven't slept in a tent since I was a boy scout and so have little to say on this aspect of travel, but like villa borrowers, camp followers are very much their own sort who already know the ins and outs of their particular mode of travel. Then there are activity holidays where the children are packed off to canoe or ride while their parents relax on a Greek island wondering whether they've drowned or fallen off and broken their necks. They're said to have a whale of a time but I'm sure they'd rather visit Legoland with their parents, when for one thing they would be able to exercise the inalienable right of children on holiday to stay up until they drop, rather than being packed off to bed because it's good for them.

Castles and ruins, if climbable, always go down well

Children travel not so much hopefully as in a state of great impatience, and it's essential to keep them amused on the way. There are various activity packs designed especially for the purpose, or you can make up your own activity pack consisting of crisps and comics; but you cannot beat the old family saloon game of spotting pub signs or licence plates or the objects of interest in alphabetical order; or, should there be no objects of interest other than cloud formations, playing I Took My Dog Shopping. I took my dog shopping and we bought an apple. I took my dog shopping and we bought an apple and some biscuits. I took my dog shopping and we bought an apple, some biscuits, and a corkscrew . . .

Going Solo

Among the advantages of travelling alone are that you can do everything at your own pace, and that one can live considerably cheaper than two, notwithstanding the iniquitous single-room supplement. Among the disadvantages are that there's no one else to blame when you get lost, no one from whom to borrow whatever you might have run short of, and nobody to share the joke when things go wrong (travel is apt to throw up those ungolden moments when if you didn't laugh you'd cry). And nobody to share the view. Seeing the seven wonders of the world somehow isn't the same if there's no one to wonder at them with you.

Travellers go solo either from choice or because they can't find anyone to go with them. They're not necessarily ungregarious: those who go it alone from choice may be looking for adventure on the way, the ones who do it from necessity may not know anyone who can run to the class of trip they contemplate – or maybe their partners simply have no desire to visit Greenland.

True loners head for under-populated areas such as the Andes where they commune with nature and play their Walkmans. The rest, including that not inconsiderable contingent whose sole purpose in travelling alone is either to meet someone or get away from someone or both, make for those well-marked locations across the world where they are most likely to run into their own kind. Regular lone travellers can effortlessly tune in to a network that extends from Earls Court to Sydney and back again the pretty way. The temptation there is to regard the migration itself as the accomplishment of travel: I've known Aussies who've come 12,000 miles to London and never budged out of the Earls Court Road. But unlike the general run of travellers progressing in tandem or bulk, the lone wolf, given the initiative, has the opportunity and the incentive to get to know some of the natives and penetrate the tourist-trap veneer. I gave English cigarettes to two girls I met in Gorky Park and they took me dancing. That beat the visit to the exhibition of folk art Intourist had lined up for me.

Women venturing abroad alone do not have it easy. Indeed, they do not have it easy in their own country where, while things have begun to improve with more and more business women travelling, there are still barmen who treat them like hookers and waiters who stick them in the remotest corner and then ask patronisingly if they realise the half-bottle of Frascati they have ordered is not a sweet wine. But if they thought Britain was the bastion of male chauvinism, they have only to cross the Channel. The belief that unescorted women travellers are easy pickings, on the game or otherwise no better than they should be, begins at Calais and progressively hardens the nearer one gets to the equator, via Italy. (The colder the clime – Germany, Scandinavia, Iceland – the more respect there is for the independent woman – except in the international hotels where, as in international hotels the world over, she stands every chance of being taken for a prostitute.) The more the local culture demands that men treat their own women like chattels, including those western cultures where the wives are treated like chattels on a pedestal, the more vulnerable is the lone woman traveller. I am told that it helps to wear over-modest clothing, sport a wedding ring and avoid all eye contact, but that if the choice is between the Middle East and Middlesbrough, a lady should choose Middlesbrough.

Which is ridiculous. One solution for the woman travelling alone is not to travel alone at all, but presumably she's thought of that and rejected it. Another is to join a tour, when she can keep herself to herself as much as she will, though there is bound to be at least one lecher on board. But at least the entire Middle East will not be as the forbidden city of Mecca.

Non-intrepid solo travellers of either sex, indeed – for so far there has been a touch of the back-pack in this discussion – might consider the organised tour as a means of getting abroad without the prospect of there being nobody to talk to except the statues round the fountain. If they've considered the idea and given it the thumbs-down, it could be because of fears of being a holiday leper among a crowd of happy families and jolly twosomes, being assigned the worst and smallest room in the hotel and charged double for it, and being made to eat at a cloth-covered card table next to the swinging kitchen door. But nowadays there are tour operators who acknowledge the existence of single travellers by waiving single-room supplements and encouraging the lone traveller to the point where you will not be made to feel like the Hunchback of Notre-Dame on his annual hols. Ask your travel agent.

Then there are single holidays. I am not thinking of those frightful rave-ups you see advertised on tube stations, which are to travel what the disco is to ballroom dancing. For 'the independent over 30s' (which I think means the under 55s) there is at least one organisation, Solo (Holidays), 41 Watford Way, London NW4 3JH, which arranges holiday groups from the English countryside to Venezuela in a well-balanced mix by age and sex.

Finally there are cruises. See *Ways and Means* for what little I have to say on the subject, but remember the maxim that the longer the cruise, the older the passengers.

I wouldn't mind seeing China if I could come back the same day.

PHILIP LARKIN

133

Business Class

Stray late at night into the bar-lounge of one of those mega-hotels where you don't know whether you're in Rotterdam or Rome, and you will find yourself surrounded by sober-suited chaps unfurling computer printouts from their black executive briefcases or huddled over their Filofaxes as they go over tomorrow's gruelling schedule.

. . . the belief that unescorted women are easy pickings

These are travelling businessmen, who according to legend should be in a nightclub at this hour with their arms around a couple of hostesses. HM Government, whose balance of payments figures they are bumping up by the minute, compounds the mythology in the most insulting way by issuing crass full-page newspaper advertisements cautioning them to keep away from call-girls. The truth is that most of our businessmen abroad are far too whacked

134

for that sort of thing and far too tensed-up to unwind with more innocuous diversions.

Unless they're very big wheels indeed, when their local minions will lay on lunch at the lakeside restaurant and a box at the opera, most visiting firemen are lucky to see more of the passing show than may be glimpsed from the revolving restaurant atop their hotel. Not that they mind: when travelling businessmen swop notes it is not on the finest beaches or the delights of the Chinese quarter, but on which outfit is offering the best fly-and-drive deals, where the cheapest duty-frees are to be picked up, and which airline has the most generous frequent-flyer bonuses. If, in their Hong Kong suits and Cyprus shirts and flashing their fake Cartier watches, they sound not unlike motorists discussing the best way of circumventing the holdups on the M25, this is their shoptalk and they revel in it.

Established business travellers (as distinct from commercial travellers, who never see an airport except from the motorway) know all the ropes already and need no advice from me. For those about to embark on this strange form of life, I have but two recommendations over and above those here offered to the general traveller.

The first is either to take out a subscription or to get on the office reading list for *Business Traveller* (388–396 Oxford Street, London W1N 9HE, tel: 01-629 4688), which is by way of being the business equivalent of *Holiday Which?*, crammed with hard-fact airline and hotel surveys, insider reports on cities across the globe, and breakdowns of such essential data as world comparative prices of whisky, all written by travel-stained veterans who know their stuff. I hasten to add that I have absolutely no connection with this publication.

Secondly, and equally importantly, it will richly reward the fledgeling business traveller to seek out and suck up to the lady we will call Miss Golightly. Every big office has a Miss Golightly. She it is who makes all the travel arrangements. Miss Golightly, while nice enough when stroked the right way, has a puritan streak which secretly disapproves of executives knocking back the king prawns in Cathay Pacific's first class when she herself has to pig it in economy and no further than Spain at that, unless she has worked a freebie through the office travel agent. More to the point, Miss Golightly has power. Cross her, and she can make your life hell. You will find yourself routed to New York via Athens with a three-hour stopover, bumped down to steerage when first and club class are all but empty, stranded on standby at Anchorage, landing at Kuala Lumpur with a connection so tight that it can only be met by abandoning your luggage.

So be nice to Miss Golightly. Find out her birthday and bring her flowers. Send her postcards. Know her size in everything and always return to base with a present. Ask after her cat. Bring her cat presents. It will pay dividends.

Should it be up to you to make your own travel arrangements for business travel, and you're at liberty to pick your own travel agent, find someone small enough to need your business but big enough to have all the right contacts, and cultivate him. Take him to lunch. He will get you the best ticket deals available and smooth your way into the magic circle of favoured passengers who stand to get bumped up to superior seats when space is available. On this last score it is not a bad idea, either, to find out the name of the public relations director of the airline you travel most on, and write and tell him when you've had an unusually good flight. If you've had an unusually bad flight, let your travel agent do the grumbling. But don't bring Miss Golightly into it. Butter her up though you may, you can't really expect her to sympathise because your flight ran out of champagne before it was off the runway.

*The only way of catching a train I ever
discovered is to miss the one before.*

                                        G. K. CHESTERTON

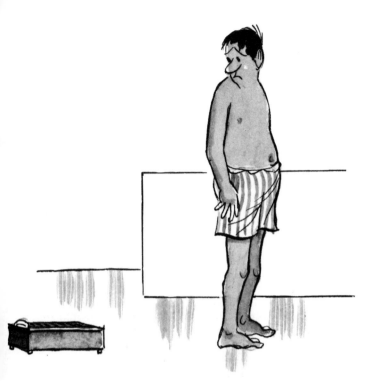

On no account weigh yourself

Homecoming

As every psychologist knows – or certainly every psychologist who has ever returned from two weeks on an island paradise to a cold house smelling vaguely of wet flannel – the time we most need to go on holiday is when we have just got back from holiday.

Never are the spirits lower. Never does one feel quite so exhausted. Never is one so filled with remorse. All that money frittered away on good living and what is there to show for it? A rapidly-fading suntan, three inches on the waistline and a damp patch on the stair-carpet where the skylight has been left open for the past fortnight.

There are two known cures for post-travel melancholia. The first is to call a radio cab, return to the airport and take the next plane out to wherever you have just come from. The second, less expensive and more practical, is to observe a few simple steps which I have gradually formulated during a lifetime of travelling from point A to point B only to find myself, at the end of it all, at point zero.

1. Brick walls do not a prison make, nor french windows a cage. Just because you have reached home at last, there is no obligation to stay there. Nor is it desirable – particularly if it is a winter holiday you have been on and you are proposing to moon around the house in your overcoat, waiting for the radiators to warm up. Do not linger. Do not even unpack (nothing is more depressing than opening a suitcase full of laundry in a chilly bedroom). Switch on the heating system, then go out at once. Go shopping. Take your overdue books back to the library. Go anywhere. Do not return to the house until it has had time to work up a nice welcoming fug.

2. And here's a little errand while you're out and about. Go round to the travel agents and pick up all the brochures you can lay your hands on for next season's holidays. Start planning those holidays at once. Concentrate on the most exotic, most expensive, farthest-away places available. Never mind whether you can really afford a month in the Bahamas – the time for budgeting will come later. But the time for pipe-dreaming is now.

3. Back home, you must deal with the mail that has accumulated in your absence. The way to do this is to scoop all the letters, bills and final reminders off the mat and put them away in a drawer, where they should remain for at least a week. Never fear – everyone wanting to hear from you will just assume you're still on holiday.

4. Among your duty-frees there will be a bottle of that very acceptable local wine you had too much of every night, intended as a present for friend, relative or neighbour. Fetch the corkscrew, open the wine and drink it. Your need is greater.

5. *Now* you can unpack. But don't clutter the room with duty-free cigarettes, chocolate liqueurs, dolls of foreign extraction, imported musical instruments, peculiar hats or similar junk. They create the same atmosphere as paper hats, balloons and streamers the morning after a New Year's Eve party. Someone has had a good time, but it is definitely and positively in the past tense.

6. It is now time to think about dinner. Eschew the tendency of returning travellers, harassed by the hundred and one domestic tasks awaiting their attention, to tackle this first meal as if they were living under siege conditions and prepare something cold with beetroot in it. While out for your walk earlier, you should have dropped into the bank and cashed your remaining travellers' cheques and/or foreign currency. Equipped with these funds – and supplementing them with others if necessary – you should now take yourself off to a restaurant, preferably of the same nationality as the places where you have been gorging yourself silly for the last fortnight. You must drink the wine of the country, eat the food of the country, and top it all off with the brandy or liqueur of the country. This induces, or rather reproduces, that mellowness of one's last night abroad – with the bonus that you don't have to get to the airport in the morning.

7. Getting back home seems to bring out the puritan in many travellers. They seem to regard it as an occasion for turning over new leaves – all right, they seem to be saying, we've had our fun: now's the time to buckle down and rod the drains, weed the garden and perform all those other unpleasant tasks we've been putting off for months. But why should you jump in at the deep end? Return to the old routine as gradually as possible, bearing in mind that when you signed the travel agents' contract there was nothing in the small print obliging you to lag the cistern immediately you get home.

8. For at least two weeks after your return, indulge

yourself in that marvellous goat's cheese, salami or whatever that you grew so fond of while away. (You can get it, or a near substitute, from your local delicatessen.)

9. On no account weigh yourself.
10. And never forget that you have a wonderful treat in store. You haven't shown anyone your slides yet, have you?

Don't forget . . . you haven't shown anyone your slides yet, have you?

25 Good Reasons for Going Abroad

The weather is better.

The food is better – in particular, the fish is fishier, and the soups soupier.

The light is brighter.

The snow is whiter.

The people are more polite, and seem happier.

The wine is cheaper.

The architecture is more striking.

The sea is warmer.

The roads are not daubed from one end of the country to the other with thick yellow lines.

The bars keep civilised hours – and it doesn't seem depraved to have a beer at ten in the morning.

The children are more childlike.

The men are more handsome and the women less dowdy, except for the peasants and their dowdiness is more colourful.

The shops are more exciting.

The street life is livelier.

The confectionery is more mouthwatering.

The smells are more exotic.

The sounds are more exuberant.

The markets are jollier, and their cheeses cheesier.

The language is more expressive.

The nooks and crannies are more quaint and cobbled.

The monuments are more monumental.

The scenery is more spectacular, with the hills and mountains higher and the flat bits flatter.

The cars are dinkier.

The vegetation is lusher.

And so many ordinary things are different – breakfast, street signs, post boxes, the ringing of telephones, matches, newspapers, bread – that nothing is ordinary at all.

Bon voyage!

Travel Notes

Travel Notes

Travel Notes